THIS BOOK
BELONGS TO:

_____

Birth date:

_____

Birth time:

_____

Birth location:

_____

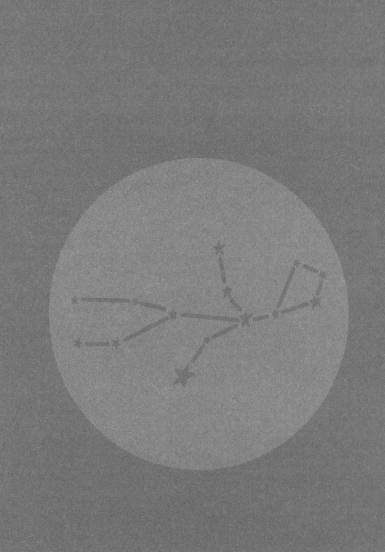

ZODIAC SIGNS

VIRGO

ZODIAC SIGNS

VIRGO

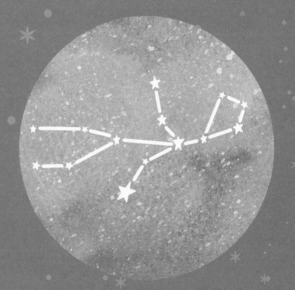

BESS MATASSA

STERLING ETHOS
New York

STERLING ETHOS
New York

An Imprint of Sterling Publishing Co., Inc.
1166 Avenue of the Americas
New York, NY 10036

ISBN 978-1-4549-3900-9

Distributed in Canada by Sterling Publishing Co., Inc.
c/o Canadian Manda Group, 664 Annette Street
Toronto, Ontario M6S 2C8, Canada
Distributed in the United Kingdom by GMC Distribution Services
Castle Place, 166 High Street, Lewes, East Sussex BN7 1XU, England
Distributed in Australia by NewSouth Books
University of New South Wales, Sydney, NSW 2052, Australia

For information about custom editions, special sales, and premium
and corporate purchases, please contact Sterling Special Sales at
800-805-5489 or specialsales@sterlingpublishing.com.

Manufactured in China

2 4 6 8 10 9 7 5 3 1

sterlingpublishing.com

Cover design by Elizabeth Mihaltse Lindy
Cover and endpaper illustration by Sarah Frances
Interior design by Nancy Singer
Zodiac signs © wikki33 and macrovector/freepik

To the memory of John Paul Matassa,
with Virgoan precision and paintbrushes

CONTENTS

♍

INTRODUCTION

Bow down. Get low. Sink your hands into the dirt and touch the life force that teems beneath the surface. Let yourself receive the subtlest shifts in the breeze. Pressure-gauge the preciousness of the plants and their readiness to rise. Know your season. Lean into the cracks and the fissures. And embrace the willingness to feel that all this perfect imperfection is just a conduit for the liberation of even more light.

Poised on the threshold between our innately beautiful bodies and how we will use them, Virgo marks the place where we pledge allegiance to our essence and divine our craft. Where we see ourselves with clarity and consciousness, standing alone and apart. Standing whole. Where we commit to the long road ahead with a tough and tender knowledge of exactly what we're here to bring, in both its contoured limitation and untamable libido. Where we decide, with complete devotion, that we cannot waste one single drop.

Often misunderstood and maligned in astro write-ups as anal, critical, and anxious, Virgo's energy is too subtle to be sound-bited, marking a pivotal moment in the process of self-development. Following the bombastic hot pink splashes of Leo's self-expression spillage, and preceding the plunge into partnership of Libra's "we-ness," in Virgo we must reckon with the edges of our selves. Who are we really, when stripped down to bare skin, sans artifice or pretense? And what do we have to give? In Virgo, we cut our teeth and slough off the excess, coming into communion with the very matter that we're made of, turning it over in our hands. Assessing and refining. Learning to love it. And learning to put it to good use.

The so-called virgin of the zodiac is not a prudish per-fectionist, but a self-contained sensualist who moves to the backroom boudoir beat of her own inner code. Reigning over natural cycles and right timing, Virgo serves as both a bellwether and barometer for microcosmic shifts in the mundane. Here to remind us that heaven is truly a place on earth, this sign gives as much reverence to the ant colony as to the castle. Ushering us to grow fierce and full with our crystal-cut capacities, Virgo energy marries us to the regalness of realism.

"What kind of witch are you?" whispers Virgo, from a cabin in the deepest woods. Work your magic, whatever its flavor, divining exactly what you stand for, and what you won't fall for anymore...

VIRGO PLEDGES OF ALLEGIANCE

These carefully crafted credos and committed principles guide Virgo through a lifetime of subtle shifts.

Integrity and Discernment

Virgo occupies the critical sixth slot amidst the twelve zodiac signs, waiting to usher us from the self-awareness of the astro wheel's first five energies and into the collective. Separating the wheat from the chaff, this sign of the apprentice is learning first to see itself as separate so it can be poised to participate, knowing its true skill set like no other cosmic cutie. Virgo's lifetime of labors is a kind of culinary art, isolating essences to divine what's most vital to the dish. But for Virgos to serve it up on a perfectly aligned platter, they must first serve themselves. And the process of tastily contributing to the world's feast begins with a deep knowledge of their own spice.

While the sign is traditionally associated with winged planet Mercury, co-ruler of buzzy, communicative Gemini, at its core Virgo pledges allegiance to the asteroid Vesta. A symbol of sensual and creative wholeness unto the self, this autoerotic aesthete is a closed carnal circuit. To develop integrity means to become integral, understanding what does and doesn't align with gut instincts. Virgo's deep dive into its own animal essence helps the sign to remain whole during the blending process, figuring out precisely what makes it tick. And developing a single-pointed focus of self-knowledge sticks Virgos to their very bones, ensuring integrity as they serve their treats to the world.

Also connected to the tarot's Hermit card in the Major Arcana, Virgo's discernment process often necessitates some real or metaphorical solo getaways, taking to a cabin in the woods to recommit to an inner knowing. There's something profoundly solitary about the Virgoan journey, even though they certainly aren't destined for isolated lives as monkish outliers. Committed at all costs to the inner sanctuary of the self, Virgos' plunges into privacy help them understand exactly what their packages contain. Knowing their contents ensures that Virgos can contribute with a sense of celebration, rather than tightly tying strings in an attempt to get it right.

Armed with an understanding of their essence, Virgos function like a fine-mesh sieve, employing a subtle filtration system as energies enter their orbit. Artfully identifying exactly what an item is made of, and how to put it to good use, Virgos must take time to turn tastes over in their mouths, touching their tongue against the "thisness" of things. Raising their noses to the world like a master sommelier, Virgo proves that their reputation for critique is actually evidence of an ability to sort the lineage of all that enters, as they apportion ingredients like members of a tasty team and play each one's essence to the hilt. Against Virgo's palate, each tasting note is an act of loving realism, and consciously delineating what's there creates pairings that bring every element into resplendent relief.

Rhythm and Ritual

Virgo season (running from late August through most of September) marks a moment when a certain form of elemental energy both reaches its pinnacle and begins to fall away. Signaling the shift from summer toward fall in the Northern Hemisphere, and winter into spring in the Southern, Virgo energy carries us across a threshold and asks us to adapt and learn. All mutable signs (Gemini, Virgo, Sagittarius, and Pisces) are apprenticing themselves to the elements, seeking to understand and integrate what has come to pass, and opening wide to what's just beginning to glimmer on the distant horizon. As with all earth signs, Virgo's adaptations occur on the material plane, showing up through the artful honoring of the body, the physical environment, and all that encompasses real, tangible life here on land.

Knowing what season of their lives they're currently in is key to Virgo's orientation and development. Deeply aligning with the markers of nature helps this sign fulfill its mission, both through their internal bodies and the external wheel of the year. For these subtle earth babes, a ritual like spring cleaning or winter hibernation can take on heightened, visceral meaning, as Virgos learn to balance cues from the environment with their inner rhythms. More than any other sign, Virgo energy asks us to pause preciously, decide our own pace and quality of movement, and commit to an unfolding that's as subtly timed as viticulture, letting ourselves remain in process until we're perfectly ripe and ready to be plucked.

The Virgo reputation for overscheduled planners and overstuffed filing cabinets is actually evidence of this process of physical attunement, as they learn to constantly check in with their place on the world clock. And when Virgos get too caught up in the agitation of constant nervous system response to these fluctuations, they're always asked to realign with nature rather than their iCals. Syncing with the cycles of the moon or following the lead of a site in the body that's holding tension helps Virgo to feel the rightness of their life force and to learn to let it fully flow through them.

When they're deep in the flow of this rhythmic responsiveness, Virgo's ritualized energies can become an ode to divine detail rather than OCD. For the aligned Virgo babe,

God shows up everywhere, and the lowliest dust bunny deity is just as vital as an angel on a cloud puff. And when they surrender their need to fix anything to their capacity to let go and let flow, the entire world becomes animated with a magical life force. As Virgo notices, separates, and seeks to refine from a place of compassion rather than harsh critique, this sign reminds itself that it fits perfectly in the wild puzzle, granting each life form its precious place as part of the organic whole.

Witchery and Wildness

Understanding the secret lives that animate the seemingly rock-solid material world grants Virgos their status as the zodiac's earth witches. Here to harness the elements for the highest and best, for Virgos to become good witches, they must learn to both read the environment's needs and honestly assess their own capacities. Working their own particular brand of magic is a process of purification rather than perfection, transforming raw matter instead of trying to make right. When focused on compassionately drawing capacities to the surface, Virgo artists can perform the highest form of alchemy, using their mettle to transform metal into 24-karat gold.

Early on, Virgos must carefully consider where to aim this alchemy, elevating their sometimes ego-effacing energy through reciprocal exchange. Rather than simply refining any rough-edged stone that crosses their path, focusing their consciousness where it's most needed also means figuring out where they feel most alive. Called to preserve the connection to their preceding fire archetype of Leo means Virgo must find a way to keep their own cauldron lit. Remembering that they have a right to feel their own heat and benefit from their own carefully loving attention ensures that Virgo's magic doesn't drift into martyrdom.

When out of alignment, some Virgos will try to do it all, standing vigil day and night and serving at altars at the expense of any sense of self. To avoid complete obliteration and behind-the-scenes burnout means Virgo must commit to becoming a conscious channeler rather than a muted medium. When they feel like they've started losing themselves in the mix, Virgos are always invited to return to the altar of their beautiful bodies. Are they constantly angry when the wind picks up? Can they read a room through raised hairs on their arm? Checking in with these carnal weather reports helps Virgos read the subtle signals of their own skin before they blindly start putting skin in the game.

As they connect with the subtlety of their bodies, Virgos are able to harness their high-functioning nervous systems for true healing work. Rather than the sign's usual association with health nut hypochondria, Virgo's fullest flower is found in the "like heals like" language of homeopathy. When concerned with paying an ode to what's here and understanding through holism rather than a nitpicky inventory of symptoms, Virgo can unleash a lusty love for all functions of our humanness. Seeing the medicine in every moment, whether astringently bittersweet and prickly, or holy honeyed, reminds Virgo that it's all part of it. And that they're a part of it too.

When Virgos learn to bless their natural appetites and embodied urges, these vestal vixens can return to the center of their own pantheon, swapping stake-burning exile for lasting self-sovereignty. Holding both the lock and the key to their own chastity belts of "shoulds" lets this sign unleash their wildness in the service of an even higher law. To know the windiness of wind on their skin. The fierceness of the flame. Or whatever their chosen flavor. To let things be exactly as they are, in all their perfect imperfection and divine discomfort. And to marry themselves to what lives inside of them, attending to the tiny biosphere of their beings with sweet, soft devotion.

This ode to Virgo's intricate intensity and subtle shifts is brought to you by the sands of the American Southwest. By latticework and lace. By the most sensitive wine grapes and the essential wholeness of butter on bread. By the sparkly specks in the pavement cracks and each distinctive star in the sky. Everything matters, says Virgo. And everything is made of matter. It's time to bring exactly what you're made of to this feast.

VIRGO

as a Child

L ike baby animals, Virgo children read the world's complexity through environmental secret language, registering shifts in the weather with their fur. Both vigilantly tapped in to all that is, and fully alive to the physical sensation of having incarnated in the first place, little Virgos are encouraged to stay little as long as possible, leveraging their youthful maturity with a less structured sense of play.

First and foremost, Virgo babelettes are observers of the natural world, other children, and themselves. After the excesses of Leo, the zodiac's previous sign, Virgos step aside from the hot-blooded playground power moves to catch some shade. And whether burying their noses in a book, or themselves in the sand, these kiddies can have something of the invisible about them. At its most beauteous and free, this invisibility cloak is evidence of an undercover privacy pact that the little witch makes with the world, and staying low to the ground lets Virgo love up on the Universe's signs and signals more deeply. But the Virgo little must also connect to a sense of unbridled wildness that comes from claiming their place on this planet, letting themselves remain a rough-cut gem that's valuable no matter its state of polish. Virgo children are encouraged to notice when they're getting pushed aside, swapping out a firm sense of self in favor of letting the other, more obvious, kids take center stage, and losing their "I" in the process.

In childhood, Virgo's relationship to "craft" gets carefully created, and these littles can think of their youth as a kind of sorcery school. Forging a relationship to the mystery of it all is critical and will lay the groundwork that keeps Virgos wondering and wandering through the world with ease, rather than anxiously breaking a sweat sorting it out. Supporting a Virgo child's body knowledge will keep them forever close to the ground of inherent instinct, a careful campground scout who both learns to respond to nature and can celebrate their capacity to start the fire.

ALL CREATURES BRIGHT AND BEAUTIFUL: THE MAKING OF A LITTLE WITCH

A kind of child-size magic mushroom trip, Virgo's life-world exposes the inherent aliveness of all beings. As Virgo children look around them, they notice even the smallest pulsations of plant life, attuned to the desires of the actual dirt and the screams of broccoli stalks as they hit the frying pan. For a Virgo youth, even bacteria can be beautiful, and early celebrations of organic processes help these little witches build deep trust in their own natural selection, the appetites and attitudes of even the trees serving as evidence that they, too, get to take their place amidst the pageantry of the seasons.

This "aliveness" can course through a Virgo kiddie's veins when they are left to their own devices, as they literally dig in the dirt with glee and put their hands on things, sorting the natural world into the sign's notorious categories as a way to celebrate their own corresponding desires and needs. Whether on campgrounds, in natural history museums, or simply having an imaginary tea party in a backyard thicket, this process of whispering to the world reminds little Virgos of their necessary place within it. As they prepare for the harder edges of adult critique in later years, these early encounters with an animistically supportive environment help young Virgo develop a core sense of self that's in conversation with all creatures bright and beautiful.

To further support the Virgoan creation of self, the little witch must seek to balance scientific inquiry into the how and what of the Universe with a lusty, full-bodied immersion in the experience. Often, Virgos will catch themselves mid-play, placing an analytical distance by creating elaborate taxonomies or staging a step-by-step experiment. And although there is nothing inherently wrong with this more measured process, evidence of Virgo's desire to understand each creature's singular specificity and contribution to the whole, bolstering the earthier aspects of inquiry keeps these little witches connected to their own instinctual navigational system. Balancing trips to the science section of the bookstore with all-out wilderness expeditions helps Virgo remember that beneath the facts, there is the fullness of life force that animates this earth and their own desires within it. Exchanges with the earth's creatures build Virgo's compassion muscle, as the sign sensitively extends a hand to a paw, looking to walk through this world, *with* this world. Like the anthropomorphic household items that support Belle in *Beauty and the Beast*, Virgo longs to both help and be helped by the matter that surrounds them.

DOLLHOUSE DIVINITY: THE VIRGO CHILD'S MICROCOSM

When they focus on letting the details wash over them, rather than trying to lock them all down, Virgo children have a veritable Polly Pocket™ of pleasure awaiting and can give themselves over to cracking open nutshells, taking apart clocks, peering through dollhouse windows, and turning over logs. As they gaze inside and underneath, Virgos gain further evidence of the very stuff things are made of, and how they function. Taking apart, putting back together, and rearranging remind little Virgos that they, too, are intricate systems. There is a deep interiority to this sign, and at this stage of development, mini curios and miniature worlds are both symbolic of their capacity to find divinity in the detail and a source of support for Virgo private lives. Yet rather than trying to micromanage these miniature worlds, or fix parts that appear broken, building trust lies in simply relishing the life that exists inside. Experimenting with acts like shaking a snow globe, rather than painstakingly picking out dollhouse curtains, can remind Virgo that Fabergé egg treasures await their tender, ecstatic touch more than their attempts to perfectly play God.

Seeking to ensure that each creature has its own clear-cut place reminds Virgos that they have a plot to possess within this pantheon. Virgo kiddies benefit deeply from divining their own spatial contours and having their own mini turf to tend at home. Whether an Easy-Bake® Oven re-creation of their parents' kitchen, or a secret spot under the stairs where they store their most prized possessions, a personal domain helps Virgos regain their center and stave off some of the overwhelm that can come from the wildness of the macrocosmic world. The "too muchness" of it all is mitigated by their mini habitat, and prideful possession ensures that the critical impulse doesn't extend into other family members' closets.

And as the little Virgo moves out from these more private places under the stairs and behind the bookshelf, a sense of tending turf continues to keep them steady. Young

Virgos come alive when watching over microcosmic plots of land, delighting in window seed boxes, veggie garden plots, and sea monkey colonies. The classic grade school egg baby project, where partners incubate an almost-hatched creature, was designed for Virgo youth, and in this endeavor the sign discovers that the capacity to care *for* is just as vital as being careful. These kinds of natural world management assignments satisfy some of Virgo's desire to both tweak and refine, but ultimately remind the little witch that there is a wild inevitability to nature that they must bow to, moving rhythmically with what is forever untamable.

NURSE'S OFFICE SOVEREIGNTY: BUILDING A VIRGO CHILD'S BODY KNOWLEDGE

The Virgo child is a deeply feeling creature, affected by the most nuanced changes in their own and the collective's proverbial skin. These tiny zodiac babes are vessels and lightning rods, running the whole of existence through their bodies without the Virgo adult's finer-tuned filtration system. Rather than writing off a young Virgo's sensitivities to scratchy fabrics and strong smells, these can be used as kinds of scavenger hunt points of inquiry, letting Virgos learn where their bodies end and the world begins.

Unfortunately, because we tend to immediately pathologize many forms of body knowledge, these little environmental readers may end up in the nurse's office, convinced that their earthy sensitivities are a sign of sickness rather than their own burgeoning capacity to heal. To keep the Virgo babe from getting locked into a hypochondriacal cycle of illness and treatment, they're encouraged early on to find ways to read the language of their bodies beneath the noise and to speak these secret signs into being. Is the grumble in their gut really evidence of a stomachache? Or is it telling them that they don't want to play this game anymore?

Building a body language reminds young Virgos that operating from their gut is always better than short-circuiting clear signs to avoid creating a mess. *Everybody Poops* should be on every Virgo kid's bookshelf, a reminder that venerating all parts of their humanness liberates self-compassion and soothes self-critique. As they get closer to the carnal, Virgo kiddies remind themselves of their right to instinct and appetite, staying close to their wildness without having to treat it. Even if these little cosmic cuties might not pull an all-out fire sign tantrum, or bite playground arms like a Scorpio, Virgo youths are invited to let the tears flow freely without needing to constantly contain themselves. Moving bigger feelings of anger or sadness out from the background can help Virgo's litany of allergies and body ailments start to heal all on their own.

For those who parent them, it's critical to attend to this child's instincts by not forcing them to engage in activities where they evidence strong aversion. While developing some risk tolerance is vital to avoid becoming the boy in the bubble, responding to intuitive hits not to plunge into the kiddie pool headfirst or ride the roller coaster helps young Virgos find their rudders. Pleasure rests in powering up with a private definition of play, rather than getting tug-of-warred into submission. Whether through solitary play or long, idle afternoons spent tea-partying in the woods, Virgo's overtaxed nervous system is soothed when self-governed, wedding these wee ones to their own forms of fun.

LEMONS INTO LEMONADE STANDS:
BALANCING PLAY WITH PRAGMATISM

Virgos' inherent desire to be of use can come on strong at an early age, and they may take a special delight in dressing up in their parents' work clothes, setting up shop in their rooms, or running a neighborhood library out of their own book stacks. These microcosmic experiences of future labors are certainly something to be celebrated, evidence of the pure pleasure a young Virgo can take in sorting and serving. But they're also prime opportunities for learning to sort the difference between the tiny Virgo's sense of the external world's shoulds and a deeper inner authority. Knowing that they don't have to make good to be good ensures that the little Virgo can play the proverbial "game of life" with a more relaxed panache, delighting in rolling the dice as much as they do advancing through the stages.

Balancing these energies can start with injecting some color into household chores. Even on summer vacation, these littles love a to-do list. As they delight in polishing a bathroom mirror or carefully laying out the cutlery, they're encouraged to bring their own signature sense of artistry to this process. Whether it's creating abstract shapes out of the cutlery, rather than having to lay out the pieces in the proper order, or leaving a note etched onto the corner of the mirror's fog, finding themselves reflected in their work at a tender age ensures that they remain devoted to their own process, choosing to engage in labors of love rather than constrained by soul-dampening diligence. And while wee Virgos certainly shouldn't be forced to shut down their paper routes, saving a space for more outright forms of play lets them start to surrender to some of the mystery without having to map it all out.

Young Virgos are encouraged to remember that they can choose their own adventures rather than always following the box. Repurposing household items as toys or staging treasure hunts where they craft the clues, instead of having to seek and find, reminds Virgos of the delight in the unfolding. By choosing to occasionally forgo organizing the sock drawer in favor of making a sock puppet instead, Virgos learn that the existence of all things, including themselves, is a gift to be cherished rather than a surface to be polished spotless.

VIRGO

as an Adult

As the little witch leaves sorcery school and starts to work more mature forms of magic, there can actually be a sweet sigh of relief. Young Virgo's sense of seriousness doesn't always sync with the playground antics of youth, and for some of these sensitive souls, the boundarylessness and "searching" quality of early life can feel like a deluge of infinite possibilities for their sieve to sort. As the constraints of time and space close in, Virgos can relish treating their life like a self-driven haiku, each adult decision a chance to refine their careful filtration system. Whether picking out the curtains for their new apartment or deciding definitively to leave a lifelong habit in the dust, Virgos find increasing serenity in the solidity of their hard "nos" and full-on "yeses." Aging gifts these beings the opportunity to drop into alignment with their very bones.

Amidst the endless responsibilities of adulthood, the Virgo delight in daily divinity takes even deeper root, and the sign savors both what it can do by itself and for the world. From refining the grocery list by their own hand to growing herbs in the garden in conjunction with the shifting temperatures, adult Virgos dance between inner examination and self-selective service, building increasing trust in their competence when meeting external conditions. Adult Virgos are constantly calibrating, checking to make sure the outer matches their inner code, and the process of maturation finds them increasingly employing their sieve, sifting through the dirt to pan for precious metals and deciding exactly where to send their efforts.

At its most gorgeously expressive, Virgo adulthood is a viticultural process, with Virgo's heart and soul-shaped grapes spending a lifetime gaining specific terroir. How will Virgos move with the rhythm of the unfolding seasons? What flavor profile will they take on as they expose themselves to the elements? What experiences will alter their chosen altars? What essence will remain? And how can they trust that they'll gain value and sheer deliciousness by simply exposing themselves to the weather that's there, harnessing whatever arises in the name of beautiful usefulness? In the end, successful Virgo adults are the sorceresses who know how to take a sit down at their own tables, complete with goblets full of juice from the grapes they've so carefully grown.

THE TWENTIES: CHOOSING THE CURTAINS

As young Virgo heads off to college or into the workforce, the first tastes of freedom contain an interesting paradox. On the one hand, this sign can embrace young adulthood in all its finery, leaping to fulfill the role by staging elaborate grown-up murder mystery dinner parties and caretaking more careless friends. This flavor of Virgo growing up may seem startling to those who've known them as a child, as Virgos seize any opportunity to exercise more bold forms of control. In their twenties, Virgos are sketching the floorplan of their lives with increasing detail, and they can take intense care making sure to set it up just so, convinced that where they put the coffee table is the secret to burgeoning success.

This flavor of Virgo young adulthood carries all the markers of Virgoan majesty, as the sign shapes and sculpts its world, finally getting to make strong aesthetic choices in their spaces and their lives. But there is also a wildness that lurks beneath the surface, moving at its own pace and in accordance with private pleasures. While the twenties Virgo might not always be given over to all-night ragers in quite the same style as their fellow young cosmic bucks, they can have a quiet ferociousness in their calls for freedom at this time. This young wolf will often stray from the pack with a self-contained silence that answers to no one, finding endless joy in disappearing for a secret weekend love affair or diving fully into a cryptic new hobby turned obsession that consumes them completely.

Virgo's late twenties lead toward the notorious Saturn Return transit in astrology, a cosmic moment that asks us to reckon with the structures we've inherited and created and decide how to live our lives with increasing consciousness and self-sovereignty. For the earthily attuned Virgo, this astro event might not rock the boat as fiercely as it does for some of their zodiac compatriots, already gifted with the ability to see the contours of their lives with clarity. But no other sign is so quick to make do with whatever conditions are here, powering through with pragmatism and doing what must be done. And at this crossroads of young adulthood, Virgos are invited to take this moment to reflect on exactly what gets their sweet loving attention, examining the true function of the flames they're beginning to tend.

THE THIRTIES: FEELING THEMSELVES

As Virgo slides out the back end of the Saturn Return, there can be a flavor of retreat that characterizes the early thirties. Virgos know something secret about their insides at this juncture. They've seen glimpses of their bits and pieces on the cutting room floor. And they understand how to better calibrate their carnality and creative force, choosing what's intrinsically right for them, rather than blindly doing the right thing. This distinction is critical during the early thirties, as Virgos are asked to return to their gut instinct navigation systems, using their notorious sensitivity to follow their own form toward function.

Whatever work they've chosen gets called into question at this time, and the early thirties Virgo is invited to really examine the legacy they're starting to craft. For the Virgo who has remained relatively behind-the-scenes during the first part of life, this can be a moment to consider stepping out onto the stage, speaking up in an important meeting, and finally penning their name to their carefully executed work. The rote machinations of service without specialness start to taste stale, and thirties Virgo is called to remember that they have a right to exist in the first place, using their voice to ask for what they want, need, and inherently deserve.

As the late thirties dawn, Virgos enter into the Pluto Square astrological aspect. The planet of underground power struggles and purging past patterns can expose where Virgos have given away their potency, bowing down to a cause or fellow creature possibly not worthy of their bootlicking devotion. Depending on how carefully a Virgo has attempted to keep life clean of messy carnality, these more animalistic urges might feel like an unleashed team of beasties busting out from under the bed. But if Virgo can let the impulses arise, curiously greeting them like any other crawler in their garden, the late thirties can serve as a very human reminder of their right to have an appetite. As Virgos learn to ride the waves of their emotional impulses like a Texas bull, they can find freedom in the shameless sweet feeling that absolutely nothing needs to be fixed.

THE FORTIES: FIT TO BE QUEEN

Armed with even more of their humanness, the early forties Virgo is perfectly poised for some healthy hedonism. Whatever impulses were repressed in their youth can come out to play in full force at this juncture. For Virgos, the forties are an opportunity to bow at the altar of their beautiful bods, loving up on how they're cut and contoured and what their cravings reveal about their very essence. Whether partnered or single, there's something autoerotic about this time, as Virgo syncs their skin back to their very bones, starting to finally believe that the reason they've incarnated is simply to relish all of existence.

This is also the moment when Virgos truly start to make good on their mission, understanding that their contribution is not a list of boxes to be checked, but an energetic willingness to come to the table as themselves. The question of "enoughness" that often plagues this sign has the opportunity for soothing here, as Virgo starts to understand their essence as vital and irreplaceable. There is something queenly to this era, and the forties Virgo is invited to claim their power as inherent, rather than proven through what they produce.

This era is also marked by the Uranus Opposition aspect in astrology, part of the midlife crisis suite of cosmic events. For Virgo, there can be a deep deliciousness to this upset, as the lists get burned and the libido unleashed. For this sensitive creature, the key to navigating these electrical hits lies in remembering their witchy capacity for environmental adaptation. Content to channel what's there, rather than try to control the direction of the winds of change, the forties Virgo can make magic out of whatever weather patterns arise.

THE FIFTIES: BREAKFAST IN BED

After the electrical hits of the sensual forties storm, there can be quite a bit left on the ground, and the fifties Virgo is urged to stay with and abide what might seem broken rather than immediately trying to sort. In whatever state Virgos find their house, the fifties is a profound moment to start trusting the process. At this point in their life cycle, Virgos have come up against their own form of serenity prayer, beginning to poetically parse out what they can and cannot change. And as they loosen their grip, they turn increasing attention toward how they might actually enjoy the ride.

While Virgos may have spent a big part of their existence plumping others' pillows and serving breakfast in bed, it's during this era of their lives that they're asked to consider what they've done for themselves lately. For a sign that's so deeply body conscious, Virgos can sometimes be remarkably estranged from more profound exercises in self-care, and it's here that they are asked to dive beneath the symptoms and to "treat" their entire systems with tenderness and affection. By committing to repair any ruptures in the body and spirit that have occurred as the result of overly harsh critiques, the process of softening to themselves can become a Virgo's greatest act of service.

This decade is marked by the Chiron Return, and this touchy-feely planetoid's release into Virgo's life reminds them of their sensitive emotional bodies, and the things that must be felt rather than fixed. And though it can feel like the floodgates are opening to all things beyond their conscious control, there can be a relief in washing themselves in these tides, as tears, laughter, and other big emotions come out from under wraps and wrap the maturing Virgo in a cloak of many colors. "Allowing" is the guiding light at this juncture, and the Virgoan credo to honor every creature's process must always include themselves.

THE SIXTIES: ESSENTIAL ESSENCE

Virgos enter their sixties with a stripped-down sensibility, back from the fifties spa of self-care with a newfound crystal clarity. This also marks the decade of the second Saturn Return, and, depending on how fully a Virgo reckoned with the first one, questions of soul alignment and outer security are up for review again. But as Virgo looks around at the contours of their lives in the light of day and starts to consider making changes, there's a shift in the rhythm of these adjustments. No longer content to just focus on the grains of sand, sixties Virgos start to explore the larger castle of lasting self-worth.

The sign's deep interiority becomes even more apparent during this era, and no matter their family situation, there's something of the hermit about the sixties Virgo. Wandering an unmarked trail into their own backwoods, Virgos are returning to the seat of themselves at this time, paying close attention to their private process and to the learning that can only come from staying close to the ground of their chosen lives. And although there's not anything bombastically rebellious about this sign's energy, it's during this moment that the fierce fealty to their inner code gets most amplified, as Virgo begins to police their plot with a ferociousness, no longer content to leak energy or love toward projects and people not 100 percent in alignment.

This is the era of essence for Virgos, and if they stay close to their own code, shoring up boundaries and exercising firm "nos," they start to understand what's essential on a soul-deep level. Releasing worry in favor of their flavor of emotional minimalism, sixties Virgos start to drop off what they no longer want to carry and pack only the feelings that keep them most alive. This may even take a very literal form, with sixties Virgo gifting away possessions in search of their cosmic capsule collection. This streamlined Virgo can feel freer and lighter than ever before, adopting an energetic and emotional uniform that is closest to their very skin.

THE SEVENTIES AND BEYOND:
A PLACE AMONG THE STARS

For a sign that is often wise beyond its years when wee, this stage of Virgo's incarnation can feel like a long-awaited homecoming. Whether curled up with their collections, or out in the world reading to children at their local library, this fine wine Virgo pairs careful intentionality with experiential knowledge and is poised to share their expertise with a wider audience. During this era, Virgos find ease in their craft, and creative flow trumps endless tweaking, as the sign lets efforts come through them, seasoned by their channel's distinctive form of magic.

As Virgo enters the seventies, exfoliating extraneous matter from their lives can feel remarkably graceful, and whatever is already receding in the rearview mirror simply slips away. This relationship to change is amplified by the Uranus Return astro aspect in their eighties, and a Virgo of this age range can find that any attempts to manage their lives are gleefully tossed out the window in favor of the sheer feeling of the top-down wind through their hair. For a sign that's notoriously sensitive about their physical bodies, Virgos can actually be quite content to age. As they watch themselves evolve, shifts in their physicality serve as evidence of their participation in the world around them, their bones an inevitable gift from and to the dirt on which they stand.

There is a kind of porousness to this time, as the maturing Virgo opens wide to the whole of the physical world and lets themselves be moved by matter rather than carefully mapping their place. Whether wandering at the base of momentous mountains or slipping barefoot into the aliveness of an early morning meadow, these Virgos are sanding the last of their hard edges and embracing their opposite sign of Pisces's urge to merge. Trusting so firmly in their distinction that they can lose themselves to the whole, this ultimate Virgo becomes a glittering dot in a blanket of stars.

VIRGO

as a Parent

After finding their own childhood joys incubating egg babies and prepping elaborate Play-Doh® pies, raising a real live creature can feel like a Virgo's ultimate labor of carefully attentive love. And if a Virgo momma or poppa can rise to the creative challenges with both their characteristic clarity and tireless willingness to refine their process, parenting helps them to become even more human. As they let their little learn to make mistakes and keep on living, Virgo parents enter into a self-study with their own capacity for full self-acceptance.

Following the signs of Cancer and Leo, Virgo represents the final stage of creation. Virgo parents are here to assess their progeny, figuring out how their little human measures up against the big, bad world, and seeing their capacity to prepare their babe as a direct reflection of their own self-worth. For the child of a Virgo parent, this can feel like a rather mysterious experience, as the babe catches whiffs of a vague sense of "not enoughness" from their Virgo parent that they can't quite pinpoint. But there is also a deep integrity to this relationship, and the child of a Virgo knows that their parent will never fake it, forging their relationship out of real love and realistic reckonings rather than perpetual golden child status.

As their little babes bump up against the messy edges of the world, the Virgo parent can actually discover that life feels better when they don't attempt to childproof the edges of their wee ones' emotional experiences. When Virgo parents embrace their status as the zodiac's healer, here to abide with their children's bruises rather than attempt to apply concealer, parenting becomes a process of creatively accepting their contradictions. Letting their littles grow up as perfectly imperfect humans, Virgos learn that evolution is a flesh-and-blood process to be fully embraced.

THE BEAUTIFUL MESS: PREGNANCY AND PREPPING FOR ARRIVAL

Virgo's glyph, both a maiden with crossed legs and an abstract art diagram of the female anatomy, connects this sign to the literal process of incubation. Virgo energy is profoundly connected to the concept of latency, and when they're in their fullest flow, Virgos can wait for exactly the right time to release their potency into the world, making sure that their harvest is fully ripe. And no matter how Virgo parents decide to bring a creature into being, there is something of this waiting that precedes their new babe's arrival. Deciding to birth another being is never a fly-by-night whim. Virgo parents often feel the call quite young or take their time committing to the possibility, imagining how they will best fit the role.

But before Virgo dives too deeply into the petri dish, mixing up egg babies with all the care of an IVF doctor, they're asked to really *feel* the process of pregnancy or pre-arrival. For this notoriously body-con sign, the adjustments to their physical form can feel startling at first, as the pregnant Virgo scrambles to read every bit of body feedback minutiae, convinced that even minor rumbles are a sign of what could possibly go wrong. Yet pregnancy, whether for the person incubating the child or a partner by their side, is one of Virgo's prime opportunities to sync with their instinctual channel. And if approached with curiosity, this time can become a deeply sensual experience of understanding their subtle carnality and responding accordingly. Pregnant Virgos are urged to let themselves be led entirely by these appetites, delighting in the strangeness of pickle and chocolate cravings, and building firm boundaries against their sensory sensitivities. If a smell or noise is offensive to the pregnant Virgo, exercising a firm no helps them gain trust in their own authority without feeling put upon by the world.

At this stage, it's also vital that the Virgo parents-to-be don't overprepare for their little's arrival, as assembling every outfit and toy before their babe has landed on the doorstep can lead to upset. While the over-preparations of their previous sign of Leo often stem from self-projection, Virgo parents' prep sometimes springs from fears of their world upending in the wake of this new being and a desire to make sure that their child is safe. But when a babe arrives in all its glorious humanness, the clothes might not fit, and the toys may end up unsuitable. Remaining buoyant in their concept and construction of their child's lifeworld is vital as Virgos learn to let birth be exactly what it is: a beautiful mess.

SOCCER MOMS AND TREEHOUSE DREAMS: PARENTING YOUNG CHILDREN

While Virgos may have spent their own childhoods in quiet contemplation at the base of a tree, the Virgo parent of a young child is urged to let loose and enjoy the unbridled expansion that is possible through unstructured playground play. Parenting beckons Virgo "backward" toward their previous sign of Leo, and these parents are encouraged to literally let themselves be led by their little, allowing a tugging, insistent hand to be their guiding force. And while a Virgo parent shouldn't forgo all discipline with their young child, carefully balancing time-outs and chore lists with wild runs through the woods is vital for both parent and child. All too easily, Virgo can start to project their own sense of structure on a wee one, and, depending on their child's sign, this may stifle the little one's simple, unadulterated innocence.

Preserving innocence in their parenting is key at this stage, and for Virgos this can start with the physical world. Ushering their babe into a garden, on a camping trip, or up into a backyard treehouse helps Virgos to regain their own sense of wonder, and lets their child see the tenderness of a parent who can sometimes seem packed into an impenetrable shell. As the two encounter the untamable aspects of nature, Virgo liberates a more spontaneous sense of laughter and strangeness, and their babe learns that the parent's high standards also include digs in the dirt.

It's also at this stage that the Virgo parent is asked to pay special attention to how much they're attempting to manage the lives of their littles, as overscheduling and excessive activity lists can be common. Keeping busy and making use of what's on hand may be a parent's factory setting, but the Virgo adult needs to remember that blank pages and idle hours can be the stuff of childhood dreams. And this hands-off approach can be extended to disciplinary measures as well. Letting their child choose their own clothes or pack their own lunch can become co-creative acts. As the child self-selects carrot sticks or picks out mismatched socks, they develop their own sense of assessment without a parent's sometimes critical gaze. And the Virgo parent fortifies their own trust that their child will meet the basics of survival, fed and clothed without every last thread stitched by Virgo's careful hand.

MEAN GIRLS AND SUMMER JOBS: PARENTING TEENS

Whether or not Virgo parents let themselves embrace full-on adolescent explorations in their own youth, as parents of teens, they are invited to remember that sneaking out the window can be as vital a rite of passage as a summer job. For the Virgo parent at this stage, there can be the initial impulse to force their kiddies onto an accelerated growth track, telling elaborate tales of their own long walks to school in the snow, and imposing a rapid-fire coming of age–consciousness through ambitious activities and internships. And while money management skills and AP classes needn't be abandoned entirely, parent and child are both encouraged to see equal value in school dances, tailgating, and making out in the bushes.

The question of "rebellion" looms large for the Virgo parent of a teen. Depending on their own teen experiences and the temperament of their child, ensuring that their kiddie is able to go a bit wild, within reason, can be healing for both parties. Underlying the Virgoan sense of hypermanaged control, there is a deeper capacity to let go and abide, feeling into the earth's natural laws and rhythms. And during the teen years, this capacity to release may be severely tested. But each time Virgo hands over the keys to the truck or extends their child's curfew by an hour, they are bolstering their own precious trust in the Universe. Not having to take care of everything becomes the most profound act of care, and the loosening of the reins lets both parent and child feel the exhilaration of the bareback ride.

As their children brush up against the gossipy school bathrooms and hyper self-awareness of adolescence, Virgo parents are also encouraged to tread very carefully and compassionately through this landscape of self-critique. And ensuring that their kiddies are free to be exactly as they are might mean facing some of their own self-image issues head-on. Whatever is happening inside a Virgo parent, they're asked to police how they present some of their own embodiment narratives at this time. Putting away their own magnifying mirrors, skin creams, and negative self-talk lets their progeny, however pimply and bespectacled, learn to love their bodies without remorse.

A FINE WINE FRIENDSHIP:
SEPARATING INTO ADULTHOOD

There can be a sense of relief for the Virgo parent as their child heads off to school or work and the contours of their selfhood seem clearer. Now, the boundaries appear more fixed, and they can start to enjoy truly getting to know each other as distinct entities. Care should be taken not to meddle in their maturing child's life, standing back to witness their kiddie as a singularly expressive being who's learning to live with their own consequences, rather than crafting elaborate rituals to shield them from the big, bad world. Yet not having to micromanage anymore can feel surprisingly refreshing, and many Virgo parents are able to actually embrace an out-of-sight, out-of-mind approach to the endless worries about their adult child's safety and whereabouts.

Depending on how deeply they've tucked themselves behind the curtains during the course of their child's life, this can lead to some interesting adult revelations. It's not uncommon for a Virgo parent to experience a kind of unmoored renaissance once their kid has been dropped safely at the dorm's door, and plunge into their own process with everything from a new hobby to a torrid love affair. And on the flip side, there can also be profound empty nest feelings at this juncture, as the Virgo is left without their carefully crafted role, no longer knowing who and what to serve. As the Virgo wanders the seemingly hollow halls of the abandoned house, they're encouraged to see this time as a vital part of their own creative process. Letting the space feel bare can invite the next hit of inspo, as the Virgo parent awaits instructions on their solo mission.

At its best and brightest, this time can lead both into a lasting friendship that springs from profound respect, as their children become intrigued by these somewhat enig-matic beings who've lived their own lives largely behind the scenes during the child's youth. Of all the zodiac's parents, these elders can be some of the most satisfying to know as "just people," with the pair finding deep satisfaction on parent/child wine tasting trips, neighborhood wanders, and long chats by the fireside. Like any fine food flavor, Virgo gets even better with age, and both child and parent can enjoy the tastes of this process with each passing year.

ELEMENTAL PARENTING

Whether you're the offspring of a Virgo who's looking for guidance on how to better connect or a Virgoan parent searching for the most star-studded approach to rearing your little one, use the elemental guide below to make the most of your lineage.

Fellow Earth Signs (Capricorn, Taurus, Virgo)

These parents and littles have it on lock, enjoying the sensuality and stability of organized toy cabinets and elaborate tea parties. Parent and child both tend to get easily immersed in habit patterns and are encouraged to save room for more spontaneous forms of fun. A Virgo parent's growing edge lies in helping their little one trust their instincts, ensuring that the child can find their navigational system without Virgo stepping in to chart their course. And for the earth sign child, they're asked to retain some of their innocence while inside Virgo's carefully crafted container, balancing their own urge to grow up fast with finger painting freedom.

Water Signs (Cancer, Scorpio, Pisces)

Both "yin" energies that are concerned with receiving and adjusting, this elemental mix can feel quite private, with parent and child regularly closing and locking doors to remain inside their own sensitive processes. For the Virgo parent, learning to respond to the subtle feeling tones of their watery kiddie is encouraged, without needing to fix or explain their child's more intense emotions. And for the watery babe, they're asked to let themselves lean against their more stalwart parent, expressing their emotions freely without fear and letting themselves be hugged and held, even when it feels like their Virgo parent doesn't fully understand.

Air Signs (Libra, Aquarius, Gemini)

Air sign children can bring out Virgo's Mercury rulership, with the Virgo parent polarizing toward heady intellectualization and analysis rather than embodied feeling. Both parties' nervous systems are electrified, and talking it all into oblivion is common. The key for both lies in balancing rapid-fire intellectual banter with moments of pause for deeper self-reflection. The Virgo parent is called upon to let the air kid experiment and screw up, releasing rightness in the name of the air sign's urges for experiential learning. And for the air sign babe, embracing some of the Virgo parent's perceived conservatism can teach these kiddies to create solid launching pads for their more far-flung visions.

Fire Signs (Aries, Leo, Sagittarius)

A deliciously challenging collision, fire babes bring a wildly irrational, larger-than-life fantasia to Virgo's more regimented world. Common ground is found in the sheer willpower of earth and fire, as they combine to further shape both parent and child's sense of creative confidence and self-sufficient competence. For the Virgo parent, the growing edge lies in letting their little live it all out loud, staging whatever drama they need without Virgo having to clean it up or tamp it down. And for the fire sign babe, they're learning to live with Virgo's fine art of creative constraint, letting the Virgo parent's imposed limitations and need for privacy be read as labors of—rather than lack of—love.

VIRGO

in Love

There is arguably no area more misrepresented in pop astrology than Virgo's love and sex life. And the intricate complexities of the zodiac's harvest maiden reveal that their so-called "virgin" status is anything but prudish. This woodsy witch is romantically self-possessed, filled with a coiled, self-contained potency that stirs her own carnal cauldron first and doesn't give it away freely. In love, Virgo's keyword is *devotion,* and whether choosing to literally bow down in a BDSM-infused affair, or approaching the altar of monogamy clad in white, Virgos must consider exactly to whom and to what they are serving up their hearts.

Before the symbol was coopted by the patriarchy, Virgo energy was steeped in the goddess, an archetype that simply meant "whole unto herself," rather than chaste. Virgo's notorious choosiness is further evidence of a fierce inner code, and high standards certainly don't rob this sign of sexual libido. In fact, when Virgo energy is fully connected to its carnal center, there can be a full-on feast of the body's functions. Collapsing the categorical divides between virtue and vice, this ripe-when-ready harvester celebrates the organic urges and delicious quirks of the human animal in love.

Choosing an appropriate altar for their ardor can be the work of a lifetime, and in all partnerships, there's some degree of sweet solitude to Virgo's journey. For any friend or lover who lives by Virgo's side, understanding this loner status is critical to sustaining their collision. While it may not make itself explicitly manifest through literal get-aways and disappearances, there is a part of Virgo that will never belong to another being. And once both Virgo and their beloveds embrace this most personal locket that lives inside the sign, they are gifted with a devoted partnership that lets both of their hearts live, coming together through the separateness of two selves that are truly seen.

JUSTIFY MY LOVE: DATING AND COURTSHIP

Because of the sign's more subtle heart songs, the fast food of modern dating can sometimes feel abrasive. Virgos crave carefully crafted companionship and elaborate tasting menus, and swiping right and then showing up to an amorous job interview often feels remarkably boring. But as the single Virgo navigates the dating wilds, they're asked to balance between their high-end selectivity and a little bit of spontaneous fun, letting even bad dates become natural history experiments. While a dating Virgo doesn't have to completely relax standards, allowing for the possibility that a future lover might arrive in an unexpected package lets Virgo loosen the controls and discover what actually turns them on.

When they're attentive to urges that lurk beneath societal trappings, Virgo's inner code can sometimes lean decidedly kinky. Even inside the white wedding Virgo dreamer, there can be something deliciously sordid, and Virgos are encouraged to connect to this sex-positive carnal knowledge, dropping out of amorous analysis and between their sign glyph's carefully crossed legs. As they embrace a fuller range of sensual flavors, following their bodies instead of their heads, Virgos learn to move beyond the binaries, and can forge relationships that are delightfully non-normative.

Whatever partnership shape and size they decide on, the process of defining a relationship must feel personal. And any Virgo heart explorer is urged to exercise some healthy restraint when swallowing inherited love stories. As parents, friends, and popular culture urge this sign to adopt tried and true pathways down the proverbial aisle, Virgos must always walk their own way. When this sign is single, they're often scapegoated at family functions, as a pushy uncle or cousin keeps asking them why they haven't yet found "the one." In these moments of pressurized constraint, Virgo is asked to assert their amorous code, reminding themselves that love comes in as many forms as there are lovers to feel it.

Once Virgos have identified an object, or objects, of their affection, the devotional acts begin. This sign's fully focused, careful attention to a lover can sometimes lean toward the critical, skipping the honeymoon phase and heading straight into the harsh light of day. Under the Virgo gaze, a lover can become yet another candidate for refinement, evidence of potential rather than personhood. It's especially vital that Virgos in the early stages of love remain open to encounters with their own and their partners' humanness, cultivating a willingness to stay with any messy emotions that arise. When their attention is focused on the mysteries of the flesh rather than the fixable cracks and fissures, there is truly no sign better equipped to understand the intricate chambers of the human heart. Filled with the sacred act of giving themselves and receiving another without judgment, Virgo finds their higher love.

LABOR OF LOVE:
THE LONG-TERM VIRGO PARTNER

A mash-up of riding-crop leather and Victorian lace, Virgo's relationship to domesticity is decidedly complex. On the one hand, the sign may harbor hardened honeymoon visions of idealized long-term partnership, creating impossible standards for potential betrotheds who are forever falling short. But even these standards can actually be evidence of the more untamable qualities of the sign, as the endless search for the elusive "one" frees Virgo for spending time in solitude. Whatever their path toward enduring partnership, Virgos must be careful to own this seeming paradox, balancing devotion to another with sustainable self-love, checking in at every turn to ensure self-sovereignty rather than blind servitude.

As the sixth sign of the zodiac, arriving just after Leo's signature flair and before Libra's deep mirroring, Virgo represents the last moment we truly have to ourselves. No matter the style of long-term love affair they enter into, there is something of the singular bachelorette or dashing widower to this sign. While they're not necessarily inclined to wander sexually, preserving this inner flame in some form is vital for the sustenance of their longer affairs. Keeping a proverbial backroom, basement, or boudoir on hand as evidence of their own secret world lets Virgos know that there is part of themselves that will forever remain self-wedded.

If the Virgo partner can learn to see their union as self-chosen and perpetually in-process, they can create lasting trust that comes from a ready willingness to do the work rather than an oppressive sense of duty. Even in marriage, retaining the concept that both parties are showing up daily rather than being bound for life can feel like liberation, as Virgo remains curious about the unfolding instead of martyred to the cause. Any Virgo who enters into a long-term affair must feel into the evolutionary aspects of their relationship, relinquishing some of the urge to keep score for the feel good flow of give-and-take. Celebrating self-development milestones instead of externally imposed markers of relationship success can keep Virgos connected to the heart of the matter, gifting compassion instead of china, and passion instead of paper.

WITH A LITTLE HELP FROM
MY FRIENDS: THE VIRGO PAL

Their friend zone is a vital extension of this give-and-take romantic tango, as Virgos learn to live and let live, transforming their harshest inner critic into a compassionate cheerleader for their besties. While they can sometimes remain blindly devoted in romance, in friendship, Virgoan sensitivity can flair up. As a Virgo pal confronts their friends' distinctive life choices and beliefs, they sometimes read their pals' self-chosen paths as betrayals of what they believe to be right. But rather than cut and run, they're asked to stick around and reckon with these differences. Learning to voice their hurts cleanly and clearly, and to trust that each pal's life path is as valid as their own, is the way for Virgo to earn and keep lifelong comrades.

When they commit to listening to their pals without prejudice and holding space for their wholeness, Virgo friends have the opportunity to activate their potential as profound healers. Remaining careful not to ride the gossip train or give unsolicited advice, Virgos help friends make sense of it all, sorting through the pieces of their lives with surprising softness. Able to identify when friends are straying from their own inner codes, Virgos can also lend a steady hand to bring pals back to center. And as long as they remember to do so with a beating heart, rather than the stern projections of their own harshest inner critic, Virgos become beloved slumber party BFFs from dusk 'til dawn.

Wherever they identify on the introversion/extroversion spectrum, many Virgos will keep a close-knit crew of friends, selecting their team members like superheroes fit to survive the apocalypse. And although the depths of these unions don't need to be discouraged, Virgos are invited to hit the streets from time to time, embracing the partygoing circulation of their fellow Mercury-ruled sign of Gemini. Making sure to balance their urge to curate with some human curiosity, colliding with people from all walks of life helps build Virgo's faith in forging their own highly personal path.

ELEMENTAL EROTICA: SIGN-BY-SIGN COLLISIONS

Astrological pairings go far beyond good/bad binaries, and every cosmic collision has worthy treasures to mine. Follow the below for a primer on all flavors of Virgoan partnership.

ARIES: This collision of cardinal fire and mutable earth is complex, to say the least, and growth lies in exploring the concept of aligned action. Virgo is floored by the obviousness of Aries's unapologetic intentions and is here to harness some of the Ram's unanalytically bold moves. And while Aries may be baffled by Virgo's urge to serve, the Ram learns to let Virgo help them channel their flame for the greater good. Together, they bond by fully supporting each other's fiercely self-directed agendas.

TAURUS: These two earth babes love to bed down, finding comfort in simple luxuries and subtle touches. For Virgo,

Taurus's full-on abundance mentality is a balm for their sometimes nervous souls. And for Taurus, Virgo's urges toward improvement can help awaken the cow out of too-stuffy pasture patterns. Together, it's an exercise in sensual stability and carnal change, letting body language tell them when to root down into their relationship, and when it's time to till the soil of stuck grooves.

GEMINI: The quick-footed planet Mercury rules these two signs, and a partnership invigorates their nervous systems and accelerates change in both parties' lives. For Gemini, Virgo teaches the winged one that endless bits of info can add up to an inner credo, encouraging the butterfly to trust in their own voice. And for Virgo, Gemini keeps the sign spry, reminding Virgo that the shifting nature of life is cause for curious celebration. Together, they're invited to soften the urge toward over-analysis and learn when to sit back and simply let their love be.

CANCER: A decidedly internal affair, these signs slide into their seashells easily, supporting each other's desires for self-protection. Virgo is invited to take a skinny dip in Cancer's emotional waters, learning to ride the tides without an overly analytical life jacket. And Cancer is asked to come in for a landing, adopting some of Virgo's more detached perspective on their highly personal feelings and cultivating an increased ability to ungrip their crab claws. Through sharing their secret diaries, they find strength in sensitivity.

LEO: As neighboring signs in the zodiac, these two lovers represent the process of vulnerable exposure, and together they're here to explore the feedback loop of self-expression and societal recognition. For Virgo, Leo's spontaneous urges for self-possessed play can soothe the harder edges of the sign's self-critique. And for Leo, Virgo gifts the over-the-top kitten greater self-awareness, helping them understand how their fiery force is received. Together, the creative contributions can be immeasurable, as the pair learns to share their hearts and shine their light with equal parts specialness and service.

VIRGO: Virgo-on-Virgo action is an intricate affair, as both signs' inner codes collide, and the universality of their respective standards is called into question. At its best and brightest, this partnership can bring each party into deeper communion with their value centers, helping these partners separate the wheat from the chaff and divine what truly matters. Together, they're developing integrity and learning to honor each other's distinctions, balancing acts of service with self-care. Allowing plenty of solo time allows these twin souls to flame on.

LIBRA: These two cultured cuties can find happiness through haute couture and sculpture wings, delighting in the potential to craft an increasingly perfect partnership. For Libra, growth lies in letting Virgo remind them that they are self-directed beings with natural urges that can't always be intellectualized. And by embracing some of Libra's devil's advocate ability to see both sides, Virgo can start to swap narrow critique for a 360 POV. Together, they're asked to balance perfect wedding visions with the willingness to do the dirty work.

SCORPIO: As the signs that connect us most explicitly to the genitals, there's an animalism in this partnership that hones each of their emotional instincts and heals fears of powerlessness. Virgo is here to help Scorpio learn greater trust and open to the naturalness of their urges with more ease. And Scorpio is here to challenge any last vestiges of Virgo's propriety, asking the Virgin to swap playing nice for following their own heat. Together, they can unleash each other's unapologetic wildness and awaken shame-free sensuality that soothes their very souls.

SAGITTARIUS: These two mutable sign magic makers find ecstasy by staying open to the experience. For Virgo, Sag wild ponies remind them that they can spread their light through excitement, breaking boundaries, and serving in a way that honors their very essence rather than simply toeing the line. And for Sag, Virgo reins in some of their tendencies toward excess, reminding the pony that an inner life is as vital as the outer party. Together, they're asked to upgrade tightly held beliefs, always ready to adjust their philosophies to follow the shifting winds.

CAPRICORN: These fellow earth signs collide around the concept of inner authority, here to teach each other about their respective rights to rule the castle. For the sometimes status conscious Cappy mountain climber, Virgo reminds them to take breaks in the ski lodges of humility while ascending to the peaks. And for Virgo, Capricorn awakens the witch's ambition, assuring them that their self-sovereignty is allowed a stronger seat at the table. Together, embracing shifting power dynamics reminds each of them that neither needs to struggle to stay on top.

AQUARIUS: Channeling the challenging inconjunct aspect in astrology, these lovers are learning to swap urges to analyze in favor of radical acceptance. For Aquarius, Virgo's conservation mode can help the sign bring their most eccentric gifts to the world, rendering Aquarian schemes useful for a greater audience. In turn, Aquarius reminds Virgo of their right to rebel against the straight lines and to question any acts of devotion that have become rote. Together, they're asked to bring the blood back to intellectualized systems, reminding each other of their respective humanity, and the personal needs that underlie their desire to serve.

PISCES: As opposite signs, Pisces and Virgo are here to make a tender exchange, each magnetized by the other's teachings. The answer lies in balancing between helpfulness and helplessness, softening savior complexes, and creating healthy boundaries to channel a love that heals their past lives. Virgo is here to embrace the sweet sense of allowing that Pisces embodies, relaxing any urges to "fix" Piscean emotion oceans while asserting their own needs. And Pisces is here to take greater responsibility for their permeability, letting Virgo's earthy pragmatism help awaken their own capacity to self-soothe.

VIRGO

at Work

For a sign that is often thought of as synonymous with the word "work," Virgos are here to learn that they're far more than just human file folders, penned from as much stardust as Post-it® Notes. In the cycle of personal development, Virgo energy asks us to hone our craft, and this sign is invited to engage in complex forms of career witchery, ensuring that the tasks they're devoted to are best serving their whole body and soul. At the office, Virgo's very essence is on the line, and finding and cultivating their calling is a devotional practice that necessitates Virgo's full consciousness.

Associated with the astrological chart's sixth house, Virgo energy is sometimes pigeonholed into the mundane machinery of work life, associated with the 9-to-5 slog rather than evidence of our more philosophical higher purpose. In the sixth house, we learn to harness our fifth house Leo mojo and transform it into functional material, realistically assessing how we will actually paint that picture or write that hit song. But this realism is a necessary step in developing a soul-shaped destiny (which will reach its peak in the Capricorn-ruled tenth house). And as any Virgo will remind you, simply showing up is half the battle. Virgos are here to make every day count, apprenticing themselves to the professional process through practical assessment of their career capacities, and building greater intimacy with their art by staying close to the ground.

Their work lives are akin to elaborate gemstone mining missions, with Virgos extracting the raw materials of skills and opportunities and turning them into jewels, applying sweet sweat in an alchemical process that draws out what's already inherent. Yet if left completely unchecked, staying close to the ground can leave Virgos in the dirt, and the Virgo professional is asked to watch for tendencies to remain underutilized or unacknowledged. Tempering their urge for exhaustive performance reviews, Virgos can find contentment in the raw, uncut diamonds of their already worthiness, satisfied by shining their light, in whatever form. When they're careful not to equate their value with a list of completed tasks, Virgos find mastery in apprenticeship, unleashing their wild curiosity and compassionately partnering with whatever work weather is on hand.

Ultimately, Virgo's professional path is one best forged in solitude, as they learn to turn down the buzz of their so-called superiors and amplify their inner voice. While developing a craft necessitates careful honing and committed practice, in the end, Virgos are tasked with building faith in their own expertise, becoming self-sovereign sirens beckoning themselves toward callings that tailor-fit their own personal journey. The more time Virgos spend dipping into their own process, taking walkabouts on long weekends away from the office, the more they can come back to the boardroom table ready to cast a spell that syncs their bodies with their bank accounts.

CASTING THE SPELL: DISCOVERING A VIRGO'S CALLING

A creative tension lives inside every Virgo, borne from the contrast between the civilized, buttoned-up dress code and the wild undoing of nature. Before we enter the seventh sign of Libra, which is all sculptural ideals and potential perfection, Virgo leaves us to reckon with the reality of our urges, making peace with our natures so we can find the middle ground between fate and free will. This animal/mineral paradox often manifests at work, as Virgo struggles to reconcile their analytical ambition toward making good with a deeper call to just make something out of the beautiful mess, answering the hunger in their souls rather than the status quo. In order to avoid becoming the caged office bird, Virgos are asked to divine exactly how much of their effort is motivated by an abstract, anxiety-ridden "should," and how much is evidence of a deeply desirous decision-making that actually feels good in their bodies.

More than any other sign, Virgo thrives when given a proverbial "gap year" before plunging into professional pursuits, disappearing into the brush with a backpack, or simply spending a summer sitting on the dock of the bay. True contribution must spring from contemplation, and to avoid getting sucked into the rote mechanisms of day-to-day drudgery, Virgos are called to commune with this higher consciousness. No matter how much of a contraction it may initially feel like, waiting to sign on the dotted line or sleeping on it before taking the promotion is always in Virgo's best interest, as they develop a pacing and professionalism that is completely personal. Soliciting inner career advice in solitude, rather than asking around, ensures that these unwed warriors are answering first and foremost to their own calling.

In the professional diagram of potential pursuits, Virgos often gravitate toward their so-called "zone of competence" or "zone of excellence," exploiting what they've always been able to do well without questioning what they want, settling on any old job that will help the world benefit from their cleanup capacity. But the evolved Virgo worker lets themselves dance into their "zone of genius," beckoned toward what makes their pulse quicken. Virgos can easily do what the rest of us don't want to, scrubbing the dishes after the party rather than partying on. To find their true calling, Virgos must cultivate the courage to stick their hands into the cake instead of merely sweeping up the dry crumbs after the festivities are over.

Whatever field they choose to pursue, Virgos are invited to become experts, diving in and digging deep down the rabbit hole of their pursuit like perpetual PhD students. Finding their soul's purpose is a carnally led question of turf for this earth sign, and Virgos are asked to travel the land and discover the spot that is theirs and theirs alone, sometimes making complete career about-faces later in life. Their turf may prove to be an intensely specific, even quirky craft. No other sign has a greater capacity to become niche, whether creating bespoke bolo ties or acting as the world's foremost expert on a specific variety of beetle. In any field a Virgo follows, whether self-employed or tethered to a corporate ladder, they must carve out a kind of hermit cave, confident in a self-driven capacity for contribution that is irreplaceable. Following specificity rather than status markers, Virgos deepen their self-sovereignty, content to clock in by their own hand and burn the midnight oil at their own altar.

DEVOTIONAL DESKTOPS: VIRGO'S PROFESSIONAL STYLE

Once they've taken a job, Virgos are quick to hunker down, dedicating themselves, sometimes blindly, to the day-to-day and disappearing behind paper trails. This sign can take great delight in the ritualized aspects of the office, finding comfort in the dry-erase boards of tasks to be done and tasks that are completed and carefully packing beloved Lunchables® for a long day at the office. This delight in the divinity of detail is never something to be written off as superficial, and Virgos are invited to embrace the aesthetics of their professional environment. Delicious mid-morning macchiatos, the most vibrant blooming desk plant, or the least scratchy suit fabric can all soothe their notorious physical sensitivities, helping Virgos build confidence in their actual ability to get the job done.

As the sign of personal assistants and backroom researchers, Virgos can sometimes become a kind of invisible, hotel-quality presence in the office, vacuuming the dust bunnies and keeping everything running smoothly after hours without a trace. And while there's certainly nothing wrong with taking on these necessary tasks, so long as they truly make Virgo's heart sing, this sign must consistently be willing to confront questions of ambition. When faced with the proposition of moving on up, some of these sign natives will say that such markers of achievement don't suit them, content to know their place and serve their purpose, no matter how small. And while this may sometimes be the case, in every Virgo there lurks a little leftover Leo energy waiting to be celebrated and integrated, even if it's just through a mention in the footnotes. Over the course of their professional lives, Virgos are asked to very carefully assess how much of their urge to avoid accolades is true dedication to the process, and how much stems from fear of exposure.

When Virgos do meet with professional success, there can be a kind of guilty feeling that creeps beneath the surface, as they're either convinced of their fundamental unworthiness or burdened by the sensation that they now have to forever secure their place in the sun. Virgos best mitigate this performance anxiety by adjusting their relationship to the concept of progress. In their most beautiful form, Virgo's workspaces are shop classes or chemistry labs, evidence of the sign's capacity to utilize and experiment with what's there, no matter the end game. Ensuring that a Virgo is delighting in each micro-moment during an unfolding project, mixing up the elements and carefully sanding the surfaces, is the key to developing a self-driven definition of success.

PERFORMANCE REVIEW: THE VIRGO COWORKER

Here to lend a hand or pick up an extra coffee, Virgo can easily become the living embodiment of an ideal coworker. This sign inherently sniffs out what must be done and gets to work doing it without extraneous pomp and circumstance, eager to be of immediate use rather than wait around for elaborate instruction. Often functioning behind the scenes, Virgos are the office fairy godparents, depositing little trails of professional gifts, picking up the undone odd tasks, and keeping the workplace bones in place, far beneath the surface.

Perpetually poised to extend praise to another, Virgo colleagues can be boundless cheerleaders for their fellow workers' capacities. Inherently blessed with the ability to separate the wheat from the chaff, Virgos see their coworkers as precious notes in an evolving symphony, acting as energetic sieves who draw what's best in each player to the surface. And as long as they remember the humanness of these constituent parts, Virgos can make excellent managers, matching each team member to their musical ability and celebrating slow and steady artistic evolution rather than forcing results. Like a perfumer, the

Virgo boss must remember that their subordinates are delicately grown flowers to be sniffed and enjoyed as part of the mosaic of nature, rather than forcibly crushed in the name of production values.

In any collaboration, Virgo must balance some ingrained low-on-the-totem-pole tendencies with an increased capacity to claim the crown. After the explosive self-expression of Leo, Virgos check themselves, and this can often manifest through a kind of endless slog of self-imposed performance reviews, or an overattachment to external assessments. Developing an internal system of checks and balances is vital for this sign, as they learn to calibrate only in accordance with this inner code.

Easily absorbed into the office wallpaper, this sign's factory setting is often to keep their head down, following the predetermined course that was agreed upon and not asking too many questions. And all too easily, Virgos can take on more and more of the dirty work, potentially building resentment, to boot. In these cases, the Virgo worker is asked to consistently return to the question of turf, making sure that wherever they are placed within the office hierarchy, they have a highly personal field to tend. Whether it's identifying themselves as the office expert on a certain topic or pushing their edges by taking on even the tiniest task that's out of their comfort zone, this sign maps their domain through micromovements. Ensuring that they don't become mere prisoners on someone else's piece of professional land helps Virgos craft from a place of soul purpose instead of anxious compulsion.

THE COURAGE TO ENJOY IT: MAKING MONEY

As an earth sign, Virgos are here to strengthen their relationship to the material world, embracing everything from tiny pebbles to cold hard diamonds. A sign of real world adjustment and learning, Virgos are in an active apprenticeship with earning, developing a highly personal money philosophy and learning to respond to inevitable ebbs and flows in their bank accounts. To maintain the money tree magic, they must connect to the roots, making sure that both the sources of earning and objects of spending are always in soul alignment.

For many Virgos, questions of "not enoughness" in

other areas of their lives may manifest as scarcity mentality. The feeling of things never being quite right, or there always being more to do, can become a hunger for Virgo, showing up at both ends of the spectrum as either chronic underearning or a ravenous appetite for amassing more and more resources to weather the storm. But this sign doesn't have to suffer at the sacrificial altar of scarcity. Remembering that no one project or person is their "source" connects Virgo to wellsprings of abundance that go far beyond success and failure binaries. For this sign, money is truly energy, and in the face of a pay cut, client loss, or job change, they're asked to ungrip their palms and open the channel wide, letting new cash flow in from unexpected sources.

As with all things Virgoan, lasting security is found through the sensual rightness of the body. And whether they're paralyzed by the prospect of asking for a raise or stocking their cabinets with soup cans for the apocalypse, Virgos can turn fear to money medicine by remembering that they are absolutely allowed to just feel good. Following signals from the body lets Virgo read their environment, feeling rises and falls in the stock market like a storm-ready animal. As the sign surrenders to the shifts, and starts to relinquish control over the bank balance bottom line, earning is somehow, mysteriously, upped. True money witches, Virgos are able to conjure something out of seeming nothingness, and when they feel full from the inside with worthiness, they can attune to even the smallest opportunities for greater earning.

For the aligned Virgos who know they are their own source and who surrender to seasonal financial shifts, heaven can become a place on earth. Able to amass stockpiles of delicious nuts over time, Virgos take powerful pride in saving, as they carefully plan their seaside getaway or slowly accrue enough funds to purchase a piece of haute couture that's carefully tailored and built to last. And as they attend to these long-term goals, Virgos are also asked to remember to savor the sweetness of spending, careful to balance their tendencies toward someday-sacrifice with relishing the ripeness of what's right here, right now.

VIRGO

in School

ike their affection for the well-oiled file cabinets at work, Virgos can sometimes get a reputation for falling in love with the mere sight of a three-ring binder. And while it's true that the rubrics and regimens of official schooling can be a balm for this soul who loves to sort and classify, the ultimate Virgo learning experience is one of trusting in the self's singular vision. Virgo's academic journey asks them to lean into the force of their own expertise, content to swap an apple for the teacher with a pie of knowledge baked solely by and for themselves.

The young Virgo can find profound comfort in the containment of the classroom, knowing exactly when to respond during roll call and how to take their place in the buddy line, whether it's as class clown or model student. While often given over to the latter moniker, there can also be something secretly rebellious about the Virgo student at this young age. As their voracious mind constantly seeks the "why" behind every single phenomenon, they are able to push teachers and fellow students beyond the settled quality of rote memorization and into the true mysteries of consciousness. Without the trappings of societal "nos" weighing too heavily, it's at this juncture that the young Virgo student can best find their forever-sought inner code. Wed to the wildness of experiential learning, and building trust in their own window on the world, tiny Virgo students wander the land, content to pick up clues and dance with the sheer curiousness of it all.

And when not tucked into the book stacks, heading down the rabbit hole like a storybook detective, Virgo can find in schooling a vital training ground for their study of the human soul. As this sign brushes up against other students' visions and lives, they collect a veritable catalog of human impulses, all the better to allow their own to be unleashed. Whether at the cafeteria table or in the sweaty gym locker room, this is particularly true of the high school Virgo, who seems to be tacitly casting a play of characters in their minds, fascinated by the whims and wants of their fellow adolescents' personality profiles. At this point in their schooling, Virgos are cautioned to be aware of when classification trumps compassion, and becoming a catty

VIRGO

teen who picks apart everyone around them can be avoided through self-acceptance. When they learn to see the crew of kiddies around them as creatures here to contribute their specific styles, rather than animals to be vivisected in anatomy class, Virgo can find exhilaration in the wondrous strangeness of life on earth.

If Virgo chooses to head on to university, there is a veritable smorgasbord of learning dishes awaiting. With the world bursting wide open, the sign must employ its notorious sense of discernment to select a singular path, and many Virgo college students will find great satisfaction in designing their own majors, gaining confidence through self-directed knowledge and the eccentricities of their chosen expertise. And with the wider freedoms that are afforded them during this time, Virgos also come up against their inner standards and sometimes obsessional, self-imposed regimens. Without the watchful eye of a parent or pushy teacher calling the shots, Virgos must decide how they will watch over themselves. Caring for their physical and mental bodies is vital during the college years, as Virgos learn to soften some of their self-critique in the name of a self-soothing college experience, careful to always support an all-nighter with a five-course meal.

Given all the time and space they need to plunge into a self-chosen obsession, the late-in-life Virgo learner communes with the world's curios with voracious enthusiasm. Retired Virgos can easily find themselves in the throes of intensive certifications, and it's not uncommon to see even the octogenarian Virgo apprenticing themselves to a brand new field that seems to signal the start of a second career. At this juncture, Virgo's knowledge has an opportunity to drop completely out of the heady "shoulds" and back into the body. These learners are less inclined toward explicitly scientific knowledge or external markers of achievement and more likely to choose their path intuitively, coming into their identities as healers through massage therapy or herbalism school.

THE WORLD IN A GRAIN OF SAND: THE VIRGOAN MIND

Like the little Virgo child peering into the dollhouse, the Virgo learner is perpetually focused on the compact microcosm, seeking to understand complex phenomena by starting with the tiniest part. Whole lifeworlds spring up in a singular pebble or magic word, and these minutiae serve as Virgo's incantations. A kind of museum-style visible storage room, Virgos are in love with the sheer range of knowledge that exists, the intricate immensity of the physical world a reflection of their own search for their place within it. Taxonomists, chemists, perfumers, and sommeliers all find kinship with this sign, and Virgo's process of looking, sniffing, separating, and mixing is an extension of their care for every last beastie on this beautiful earth.

Partially ruled by the fast-talking planet Mercury, their minds can be remarkably quick and bright, slipping on some fairy wings and buzzing around the garden to collect and classify the nectars. When a fact is shared or a new philosophy uncovered, Virgos seek to insert it into their virtual Dewey Decimal system or family tree, finding a comfy corner for this knowledge and building out their understanding relationally. Divining the place for each fact helps Virgo understand the whole, and their brand of spiritual synecdoche harnesses seemingly innocuous bits of info as bellwethers for global shifts.

This Mercury rulership also inclines them toward wordplay, and there are many Virgos whose vocabularies are dazzlingly inventive, developing infinitely innovative jargon by the minute, embracing idioms, and crafting U.N. style, real-time translations. Translation is an interesting place for Virgos to play, as they attempt to filter, edit, and discern the most functional essence of a phrase from language to language. But there is also medicine for this sign to be found in the untranslatable, and by embracing the Inuit words for snow or the culturally specific concept of Italy's *la dolce far niente*, Virgos begin to see the mysterious potency of words that are cloaked in finery without always having to be merely functional. Along these lines, a delicious exercise for Virgos can be a game like telephone, or the experience of performance poetry, where rhythms and shapeshifting affect seemingly clear-cut intellectual meanings.

Far more embodied than their co-Mercury-ruled Gemini counterpart, Virgos have to feel it in their bones to believe it. There is a prodigious pragmatism embedded in Virgos and, if cultivated, these gut instincts can help soothe some of the more nervous edges of their rapid-fire minds. Quite literally attuning themselves to the seasons and weather patterns supports their own intellectual unfolding, and the difference between Gemini's air sign mind and Virgo's earthy one is found in feedback loops. Rather than reading a book on gardening, Virgo's embodied mind is best supported by heading out to dig their hands in the dirt, learning to play with the messy process and to find faith in the wild order of nature.

DIGGING IN THE DEADLINE DIRT: VIRGO STUDY HABITS

As with other areas of life, Virgo often dives straight into studies armed with a checklist of project requirements before questioning the larger purpose. To avoid hardening their earthiness into overly literal pragmatism, Virgo learners must stay lubricated by connecting the magic to the mundane. Taking a precious pause before beginning a homework assignment or immediately tackling that extra credit exercise helps Virgos remember the "why" beneath it all. What is the purpose of this task? What element of this assignment lights up my curiosity? Who is controlling the pacing? How would I work if there were no grades? Panning out to see the macro-motivations behind the minutiae helps Virgo connect to their own navigational system, synced up with a self-sovereign style of learning rather than simply stuck to the studious status quo.

The Virgoan penchant for tweaking and refinement can find its full flower in the book stacks, as Virgo endlessly adds to their footnotes or line edits a paper into oblivion, the underlying artistry now obscured in red pen. To avoid anxious overwhelm, Virgos are asked to experiment with a little allowing in this area, practicing by collaborating with groups where they must cede some control or turning in assignments that are incomplete rather than asking for an extension. If they're careful not to take on all the responsibility for a group effort, these kinds of collabs can become exercises in compassion for Virgos, as they feel into their team members' distinctive styles and sign their names to a project they can't entirely direct. And while some Virgos may take their tweaking to the extreme, never finishing an assignment for fear that it's not quite right or finding it far too overwhelming to even begin, practicing simply handing it over, in whatever the state, can feel like a sweet liberation.

To avoid getting stuck in an endlessly mathematical system of point chasing and linear achievement, Virgos are encouraged to allow plenty of time and space around their studies. Even though their nerves may be on overdrive when faced with a deadline, taking a walk outside or getting a massage is far better for their delicate systems than trying to push through. Checking in with the body's signals to make sure their whole system is getting fed is key, and they're always encouraged to pack extra snacks in their backpacks. Rather than a caffeinated charge to the finish line, Virgos are learning to find contentment in every step, and their study habits should feel more like a carefully heated cup of warm milk than a hastily downed double espresso.

A LIBRARY CARREL OF ONE'S OWN: CREATING A PERSONAL PHILOSOPHY

As they reckon with the seeming divide between accruing more heady facts to support their claims and feeling the primal pull of an animal intuition that "already knows," there can be a kind of splitting that emerges in the Virgo learner. Convinced that their witchery won't win them valedictorian status, Virgos often sacrifice their right brain for their left and lose some of their wild creative force in the process. Connected to their astrological polarity point of Pisces, Virgos are some of the highest intuitives in the zodiac, and their spatial sensitivities tap them into the complexities of the cosmos with every step on the pavement cracks. In some sense, their educational lifetime is a process of undoing and unlearning, as they seek to come ever closer to the original kernels of inherent wisdom they already possess.

Throwing themselves into the deep end of brand new subjects with a beginner's mind helps build trust in this intuitive muscle, as Virgos are asked to navigate based on the here and now, rather than a priori knowledge. Less preparation is always more for this sign, and stripping down to this immediacy helps Virgo gain confidence in their competence. Whenever possible, Virgos are encouraged to opt for the vocational and experiential academic path. Choosing a cooking or shop class over some esoteric philosophy keeps Virgo tethered to concrete knowledge. Virgos come alive through anthropological excursions, immersing themselves in local lifeworlds and learning from the ground up.

How does it taste? How does this material react with this one right now? How can I immerse myself in this custom without having to fully understand? Learning kinesthetically, by doing, reminds Virgos that the world's quirks and kinks are cause for celebration, and that they don't ever need to be told what to do.

As with all things Virgoan, the richest answers are found on the inside, and the sign is a living, breathing symbol of the self-study principle. Any Virgo student must keep a proverbial room of their own, whether it's a literal library carrel or a place in their consciousness where they find solitary retreat. Developing a keen sense of personal pacing, and the ability to abide the often-unanswerable questions, helps Virgo find joy in the wild mysteries of the natural world rather than the pain of endless paper cuts from the archival microfiche. If Virgo commits to communing with knowledge rather than attempting to extract it or lock it down, they uncover the magical mandala embedded in the detailed microcosm. Forgoing the butterfly pinned to the board in favor of a winged wander through the open meadow, Virgo connects to an exploratory curiosity that is satisfyingly insatiable.

VIRGO

in Daily Life

As the sign that reigns over every last divine detail, an entire tome could easily be dedicated to Virgo's daily life. Governing the intricacies of our habits and the magic of the mundane, Virgo is in a perpetual pas de deux with the particulars. For this sign, life is happening on all levels at all times, and literally everything matters. Forgoing high-brow hierarchies, Virgo descends into the trenches, giving full support to the credo that the way you do one thing is the way you do everything.

And with the right attitude and intention, everything from sorting the sock drawer to scrubbing the toilet bowl can become a high art for Virgo. As they carry out the trash in their loving arms or place a gentle grind of pepper atop the morning eggs, each act becomes a tiny prayer. At its best, this process of daily prayer elevates Virgos from OCD-ridden panics over the seemingly superficial and into the spiritual. When Virgo remembers that singular specks are meant to be savored instead of anxiously swept away, this sign can bring heaven to earth, finding meditative serenity within each salt crystal in the shaker.

BEHIND CLOSED DOORS: HOME DECOR

The concept of interior design is a fundamentally Virgoan concept, as one of this sign's key missions is to find deeper union between the interior body and the outer form. The ideal Virgo den starts with the barest floor plan and the lowest baseboards, and any Virgo lair must, on some level, be possessed of "good bones." Whether apartment hunting or building their dream house, beginning the process of nesting starts with finding twigs, considering the physical form, layout, and neighborhood environs of their given lair. This sign can take immense pleasure in digging through building records, seeking to understand the very geology and mysteries of the ground a home rests upon. And whatever their chosen habitat, focusing on the matter it's made of reminds Virgos that they are held and sheltered by the earth beneath.

Once inside, Virgo is invited to fashion their home after a deep woods retreat, allowing plenty of space for solitude, rest, and rejuvenation, while also gently inviting themselves to explore the surrounding landscape. Crafting this retreat starts with Virgo's capacity to stake a claim to a plot of land, no matter how small. Even if they're living in a crowded commune full of roomies, this sign flourishes best with some small cubby or closet where they can hang their shingle. If they're sharing space, setting up a simple room divider or screen helps Virgo keep something for themselves. Closed doors, and even the containment of cabinet drawers and jewel boxes, help Virgo remain connected to their inner landscapes, powered up by the pleasure of some much-needed privacy.

Virgos can often tend toward either end of the cleaning extreme, resigned to the chaos and given to hoarding, or excessive purgers who Kondo nearly everything out of existence, resulting in a rather clinical lair. To balance between these wild swings of excessive ordering to avoid going under and throwing up their hands and getting buried in garbage, Virgos are invited to treat interior design like a highly personal act of psychological artistry. How does the Virgo want to feel in a given room? If they seek serenity in the bath, they can build an entire palette around a treasured detail, letting the scent of lavender or a beloved bronze soap dish plant the seed for stylistic magic. Starting small and swapping design mag inspiration in favor of emotional intuition helps Virgos find both function and inspiration in the very furniture.

Whatever their chosen aesthetic, some design minimalism can soothe an active nervous system, creating literal blank space for relaxing their consciousness. The sign's Mercury rulership and earth element mean that the Virgo habitat is an intricate biosphere with constantly shifting weather patterns. To keep things fresh, this sign is often ordering and cleansing, repeating spin cycles or mopping until they drop. But instead of spending all day bleaching their linens in the elusive search for perfection, a Virgo dweller can find greater satisfaction in adopting indoor/outdoor accents, colluding and colliding with the nature they sometimes seek to tame. Planting window box gardens, attending to skylights and ceiling fans, or focusing on the patio furniture and sliding doors allows for natural forms of circulation and aeration, helping Virgo keep things fresh without getting too exhaustingly clean.

SILK SOVEREIGNTY: PERSONAL STYLE

The zodiac's boudoir denizen, Virgo connects us to the behind-the-scenes body rituals we carry out before we leave the house. And though some Virgos might eschew personal care rituals in the name of utility, this sign benefits deeply from preparing their bodies to meet the world. Spending a long evening in the bath surrounded by candles, or an extended session at the vanity table before a night out, reminds Virgos that they are worthy of all of the care they extend to others, letting them transform from the masseuse to the massaged. Paying greater attention to soft touch and private rituals fortifies Virgo's belief that they have a natural right to luxury without ever having to earn it.

Choosing the contents of their cosmic Caboodle® is a process of museum-worthy curation for this sign, and as they blend and sort their contouring kit, every Virgo seeks to define their ideal regimen. Ultimately, the sign's style benefits from a few signature staples that they'd take to the grave. In keeping with Virgo's connection to the earth, these may be sensually simple selections, favoring tried-and-true cold creams over the latest skincare trend. With scents, the sign is also encouraged to stay close to the source, swapping magazine-ready synthetic fragrance strips for handpicking a single floral or herbaceous essential oil, or creating a bespoke natural perfume blend.

Carefully cleansed, as Virgos head out into the world they're invited to remain in communion with this internal essence, taking contained comfort in a scent that wears close to their skin, a picture tucked inside a copper locket, or a piece of lingerie. These kinds of sartorial secrets help create an inner devotional channel, as Virgos can physically feel something beneath their outer suit. Even their outerwear can play with this concept of interiority, as Virgo ties on a silk scarf, sports a broad-brimmed hat and dark sunglasses, or wraps up in a cardigan. Preserving their ability to "cover up" protects Virgo's highly sensitive nature.

Some Virgos may tend to downplay the need for elaborate threads, finding comfort in a "uniform" that helps them blend beigely into the background. But developing a signature silhouette helps them strike a pose rather than just stand in the shadows. Connected to their neighboring sign of Leo, Virgos are asked to invite a little flair to their function, upping the ante on age-old neutrals. Whether it's a red lip, family heirloom jewelry piece, or statement belt, this sign is encouraged to add a spark of specialness to their ensemble, no matter how small.

The quintessential Virgo style is a blend of sixties folk singer, Southwestern naturalist, and forties screen siren, and pairing earthy pragmatism with inherently feel-good luxury helps Virgos find their stride. A Virgo of any financial means is urged to choose quality over quantity, swapping the assembly line fast fashion throwaways for a single investment piece. Balancing their desire for the containment of classical form with a little more responsive flow lets this sign breathe better. Buttoning down their button-ups, pairing a cinched waist with a maxi skirt, or matching impeccable suit tailoring with wavy beach locks or a partially undone bun reminds Virgo that getting done up doesn't have to feel stifling.

KITCHEN WITCHES: DIET AND HEALTH

The body is truly Virgo's temple, and although the sign sometimes gets a rep for hypochondria, their corporeal sensitivities should be treated with kind attention and gentle grace. Constantly shifting barometers of emotional weather, learning to read their slightest shivers and smallest itches helps this sign trust their instincts. Ruling the intestines, Virgos are the probiotics of the zodiac, restoring a careful balance to the interior flora and fauna. And if they commit to digging beneath the sensation to find the feeling, rather than immediately seeking to treat the symptom, Virgos can learn to speak body language fluently, translating proprioception into sensitive support for their very souls.

The quintessential wine tasters of the zodiac, the process of sampling, choosing, and assimilating each note of the smorgasbord is central to Virgo's well-being. Instead of following strict dietary regimens or externally imposed Michelin rating systems, Virgos are encouraged to quite literally use their noses, sniffing out the finest truffles for themselves and treating every meal like a tapas platter. Having a range of sensory selections both helps this sign order their world, ranking each item they intake on a restaurant reviewer–worthy scale of deliciousness, and provides them with greater cause to celebrate the whole of creation, literally eating the rainbow with every bite. And while certain Virgos may prefer the harder edges of the bento box or military meal dividers, they're encouraged to release some of the more rigid energies around distinction, letting their food mix on plates, or double-dipping multiple dishes without washing the cutlery. When Virgos unleash their ice cream swirl, they learn that their own singularity doesn't need to be constantly secured, finding greater faith in an inherent contribution to the whole.

Eating is an art form that can help ground Virgo's "buzz" on the picnic-blanketed ground, and the sign benefits by indulging in lusciously straightforward whole foods, enjoyed al fresco. Whether it's a warm baguette and spreadable cheese or a farm-to-table feast, eating effortlessly and rustically reminds Virgo that they, too, are worthy exactly as they are, without over-preparation. Forgoing some of the toiling over the slow cooker for a spontaneous snack that's fresh and ready, Virgos learn to see the perfection in uncooked pieces. Tracing the origins of their food and understanding the life histories of the ingredients can also connect Virgos to their sought-after sense of holism, and eating locally and seasonally is particularly important for this sensitive cosmic CSA member.

When it comes to sweating it out, Virgos benefit from nuanced attunements rather than overt muscle building. And their fitness regimen, like other realms, must be a proprietary blend of body, mind, and spirit. Energy practices like tai chi or yoga help fortify Virgo's form while easing their buzzy brains, connecting them to the cosmos on a cellular level. Artistry is vital for this sign, and opting for the subtleties of a barre class rather than the burn of heavy lifting lets their movements become fine-tuned forms of magic. Whether or not they'll take the risk and give it a whirl, one of the most fundamentally Virgoan pursuits can be found in burlesque dancing. The languid reveals of this sensual practice remind Virgos that they can decide exactly how to share and celebrate their bods, pushing the comfortable edge of exposure while saving something under their pasties that's just for them. Whatever way this sign chooses to move and groove, they're encouraged to spend some time away from the mirrored gym walls, practicing feeling their bodies on instinct rather than pure visual aesthetics.

VIRGO

UNDOING THE LACES: LEISURE PURSUITS

While Virgo may not be the most overtly leisurely of signs on the surface, they can find deep relaxation by walking the line between work and play, seeking ease in arenas where they don't have to be the experts. Hobbies can often smack of undercover attempts at self-improvement for Virgo, and in their off duty lives, they're encouraged to remember that not everything has to produce an end product, content to choose pursuits that are esoteric as much as crafty. Whether it's flailing about in a dance class for the first time, or simply mushing the pottery clay into shapes without having to perfect the pot, leisure pursuits are an ideal training ground for Virgos to "unlearn" and "undo" the laces, placing themselves in the position of not needing to know it all.

Feeding their need for subtle alchemy, Virgos bloom with process-based play that lets them incubate seeds and cultivate responsiveness to the materials on hand. Digging their hands into the literal dirt is always a Virgo system soother, with everything from weeding to flower arranging to viticulture on the agenda. With any of these pursuits, Virgos are encouraged to tap into the wildness of nature, letting their bloom bunching feel instinctive and finding release as the elements affect their plants. And as Virgos tend their plots, they're also invited to remember the feast. Growing edible flowers or sitting down to a glass of their own wine grapes lets Virgo remember that they have every right to sit back and enjoy the goods rather than just be good.

Virgos can also grow and evolve when they follow pursuits that are seemingly useless, pushing up against their endless urge for contribution and opting for pure relaxation instead. A wild night at the club is just as vital for this sign as a book club, and choosing activities where there is no external rubric of accomplishment helps Virgos cultivate more natural contentment. Embracing their opposite sign of Pisces, Virgos are encouraged to love up on life's poetry, engaging in abstract art, getting lost in karaoke numbers, or simply drifting downstream on a pool floatie. Seeking out transcendent, spiritual experiences that can't be explained reminds Virgo that magic is vital to their search for matter. Whether simply burning incense or attending an elaborate séance, Virgos get lost in the mystery of the Universe rather than green juicing themselves toward wellness.

When vacation-planning, Virgo's subtle wildness finds its place in provincial locales where they can swap buzzy urban stimulation for the serenity of nature. Along rocky coastlines in particular, Virgos can learn to embrace both the security of form and its subtle erosions, building elaborate sandcastles and then surrendering them to the whims of the sea. Dream destinations must always contain a bit of organic magic, and wandering ancient templed islands with storied mythos, sniffing the lavender fields of Provence, or dipping into the healing hot waters of Iceland awaken Virgo's sensory perception without overtaxing their systems. And as they plan their getaways, Virgos are invited to release some of their urge to micromanage the agenda and open up to spontaneous contact with the local landscape, setting out with a general idea of an area to explore rather than a schedule for crossing off sites. Wherever Virgos choose to wander, they're asked to tread lightly, letting the earth's treasures remind them of their own natural beauty and the solid bedrock on which they stand.

8

VIRGO

in the World

Virgo's journey from the backwoods of their private boudoirs and into the limelight can sometimes feel fraught. For a sign that seeks to rightfully align their internal rhythms with the wild world's drumbeat, there can be an approach-avoidance pattern to their forays. As Virgos learn to flow between making sure it's just so and just coming out with it already, they learn to step out of the shadows with greater softness and less assessment. The more Virgos let themselves brush up against the concrete and steel, the more they can buff the hard edges of their inner critics, meeting and greeting the world with all their raw and regal humanness instead of always having to await the flawless moment.

PRECISION AND PAINTBRUSHES: THE VIRGOAN LEGACY

Poised and ready to bring their toolkits to the table, each Virgo is tasked with the mission of divining their expertise. Whatever their domain, they seek to do it to the hilt, ensuring that they leave no log unturned in their chosen field. Crafting a Virgoan legacy is truly the work of an entire lifetime, and the sign is encouraged to release any gripping around endgame achievements, sinking themselves into the shifting sands of an ever-evolving apprenticeship with the Universe.

Like Leo, Virgo is exploring the principle of exposure, and benefits from some internal home prep before they slide into the streets. But unlike Leo's sky-high threshold for being seen, Virgos flourish when they're able to retain a private gaze, tasked with creating a personal compact to carry with them when they're placed in the public eye. For the more mystically minded Virgo witches, the process of imagining that they are protected by a little energetic shield or bubble as they travel helps them stay wedded to themselves during their collisions with the world. Virgos are made for a healthy bit of friction, learning to slice and dice themselves into market-ready diamonds. But during this rock-tumbling process, a jewel box to rest in is as necessary as a mallet to crush. Ensuring that they have a tiny emotional ring pillow to curl up on lets Virgos shepherd themselves through the streets in safe sovereignty.

As they debut work into the big, wide world, there is an inevitable tendency to hear the whispers from the wings. And although this can often come from the external, as Virgo is a keen observer of how others are observing them, the battle they must ultimately wage is with their own inner boss. In keeping with their Mercury rulership, this sign is asked to fine-tune their internal narratives, being extra careful with the words they're speaking to themselves behind the scenes. Every word is a potential magic word for Virgos, and taping little self-loving Post-its to the bathroom mirror can save them from some of the harsh light that they shine upon their so-called "flaws." Virgos are also encouraged to gently escort themselves into center stage from time to time, ensuring that they summon the courage to be looked at and celebrated occasionally for all that they've crafted. The concept of beholding is a sweet one for this sign, learning to simply see and be seen in beauty, sans assessment. While usually given over to ghostwriting, building a stronger commitment to autographing their artwork amps up Virgo's capacity to pen a personal love letter to the world.

BOW-DOWN BOMBSHELLS AND NATURAL OBSERVERS: VIRGO PATRON SAINTS

While the list of Virgoan critics and cultural craftspeople is long, these four uncompromising witches encompass the distillation of Virgoan principles:

ROALD DAHL (9/13/1916): Embodying the Virgoan capacity to uncover golden ticket mystery tucked into an ordinary chocolate bar, Dahl's Wonka Factory landscape of lickable wallpaper reminds us that "if you want to view paradise, simply look around and view it." Shifting from an undercover life in espionage to author children's books from inside a wooden wagon, the British writer crafted ordinary heroes with extraordinary integrity and curiosity. Dahl's giant peach habitats, everyday witches, and marvelous medicines give new meaning to the art of discovering magic in the so-called mundane.

MOTHER TERESA (8/26/1910): This Albanian-Indian nun and missionary was a living embodiment of Virgoan acts of devotional service, walking the path at her own precious pace. Although many of her efforts have been reviewed as controversial, her commitment to the "call within the call" was without compromise, as she sought to sync her internal beliefs with tireless work in the world. Canonized as a saint after her departure from earth, her feast day happens during Virgo season, on the anniversary of her death.

DAVE CHAPPELLE (8/24/73): The American stand-up comedian, writer, producer, and actor is a sharp social commentator who harnesses the Virgoan craft of close observation and critical distance to create acerbic humor about humanness. Fiercely defending his personal agenda to provoke, with a penetrating wit and a no-holds-barred clarity, this polarizing performer has stood his ground, defending the "rightness" of his right to assess this world. And in true mercurial Virgo fashion, Chappelle's wild wordplay has birthed a proprietary lexicon of terminology.

BEYONCÉ KNOWLES-CARTER (9/4/81): This untouchable mistress of uncompromising craft is a veritable Virgoan treasure trove of personal power and artistic acumen.

Embracing a multifaceted persona that is nevertheless perpetually flavored with her signature sauce, each one of her self-aware steps into the starlight is a rallying cry to "get in formation." Whether slipping into the skin of self-sovereign alter egos like Sasha Fierce, encouraging barefaced "I woke up like this" selfies, or defending lusty "put a ring on it" loyalty pledges, Beyoncé's legacy is bootylicious and emboldened, making the rest of us mere mortals bow down.

CROP HARVESTING:
FINDING VIRGO IN THE WORLD

The hermetic incantation "as above, so below" reminds us that astrology isn't just an out-there system of distant stars and predestined outcomes. Instead, this sensuous language lives and breathes, speaking to us of our participation in nature and the material world. Bringing heaven to earth, astro energies are a virtual treasure hunt, found in everything from the earth's molten core (hot-blooded Scorpio power sources) to the limits of the stratosphere (Aquarian eccentric imaginings of worlds beyond). Here are some celestial scavenger sites for ferreting out Virgo vibes.

INTERIOR DESIGN: Crafting the specific style of our internal worlds is a distinctly Virgoan pursuit, and whatever your design proclivities, you can find Virgo inside everything from self-fashioned family dens to five-star hotel rooms. Starting from the basement and building to the skylights, aesthetic continuity is key for this committed sign, showing up in the slightest flourish of a throw pillow or curvature of the crown molding. Explore this energy by divining your own design "code," mixing and matching fabric swatches and creating mood boards that align with your soul's desires.

MINIATURES: Virgo's divine details find a compactly intricate existence inside dollhouses, nutshells, and terrariums. The sign's energy beckons us to consider the specialness in the specificity, and the magic in the miniaturized, caring for the most vulnerably small comforters as much as the bombastic California king beds. Even the craft of creating minis is pure Virgo, with tiny paintbrushes and observational magnifying glasses shedding light on life beneath the surface. To tap into your Virgoan sense of itty-bitty biospheres, build your own terrarium, playing with the delicate balance of elementals as you tend to small seeds, and peering through the botanical globe into a semi-private world.

PERFUME: This everyday luxury elevates body care to a high art, blending our skin's natural essence with a carefully chosen olfactory experience that shapes our trail through the world. Whether it's a subtle sillage as we pass, or a fragrance that stays so close to our flesh that only our confidants catch a whiff, Virgo energy mirrors this cosmic art of self-defining our signature scent. Connected to the sign's earthily sensual nature, everything from crushing our own flower essences to selecting finery at a department store counter can help us trust our noses, crafting the contours of an ever-evolving self.

WINE: Containing the complementary Virgoan qualities of arbor-trained civilization and untamable growth, grape to glass viticulture is an embodiment of the evolving process of care, cultivation, refinement, and enjoyment that the sign is asked to develop. In collaboration with the conditions and materials of the local terroir, wine reminds us that we don't have to push our agendas, letting the land do its work upon us and creating a distinctive flavor by channeling the elements. Tap into Virgoan delicious discernment at a vineyard wine tasting, where you can both distinguish each note with poetic clarity and just enjoy the juice at the end of all that loving labor.

WEATHER: An ever-shifting atmosphere of Virgo wildness and witchery, the weather reminds us of both our inability to ultimately control anything and the devoted competence we develop when we commit to meeting the moment. From the tiniest rain droplet to the whole hurricane, Virgo starts with a singular contribution that coalesces into world-altering work. Inherently tied to the shifting wind and sand, this sign's adaptive energy invites us into organic connection with both nature's beauty and its brutality, raising our upturned palms to the sky's reign. And when we step outside and feel whatever is there on our bare skin, we learn to handle all the seasons of our lives with serenity and strength.

CONCLUSION

Now that you've encountered the intricate inner workings of the zodiac's singularly sovereign witch, it's time to head out into the wondrous woods. Whether you're a Virgo Sun sign who's looking to re-up your commitment to your mission or a Virgoan aficionado building more trust in your integrity and personal process, follow the energy checklist below to tend your inner flame.

INTEGRITY. Are my thoughts, words, and deeds consistent? Do I do one thing like I do everything? When do I come out of alignment with what I know to be true and why? What is my personal code of ethics, borne of my own experience?

DISCERNMENT. Where is my energy leaking? In what situations and partnerships do I feel more drained than filled? Where do I want to say no, but keep saying yes? If I could curate my life exactly as I envision, what would it look like?

RHYTHM. What "season" of my life am I in right now? How do I respond to change? What geographical place connects me to the feeling that I am part of the natural world? How can I respond to the rightness of timing, rather than just pushing my agenda?

RITUAL. How does my daily routine support my wholeness? How do I care for my beautiful body? What alterations could I make, however small, to honor this life of mine? How does my personal environment (home, food, clothing, and so on) reflect my values?

WITCHERY. What kind of magic am I capable of? How can I make something out of what's presenting itself in my life? What needs to be altered or shifted right now? How can I build faith in what I cannot see?

WILDNESS. How do I honor my need for solitude? What area of my life or my self belongs to me and me alone? What parts of me will forever be untamable? How can I choose my wants over my shoulds? What would taste most delicious to do right now?

VIRGO IN YOUR BIRTH CHART

Whether or not you were honored to be born under the sign of the witch, Virgo's earth powers are for everyone. Here's how to connect to your turf, no matter your sign.

Virgo Planets and Placements

When you look up your birth chart, you'll discover that you're not just your Sun sign, but are composed of an array of celestial cuties, each symbolizing a different part of your life force and penning your personal cosmic story. First explore if you have any other planets or placements in the sign of Virgo.

VIRGO RISING: The Rising sign is the kind of packaging we arrive in. It indicates the energy of our approach (the lens we use to view the world) and calls on us to take this sign's principles to a deeper level. Virgo Rising babes naturally approach the world with a microscope in hand, carefully waiting on the sidelines before leaping in, eager to understand how they might better fit into the whole. Virgo Risings are asked to pay special attention to their inner code and outer world, making sure that they stay true to themselves on all levels.

MOON IN VIRGO: The moon is a tucked-in shellabration of our inner worlds, symbolic of how we feel and what makes us secure. In Virgo, the moon carefully adjusts itself to every fluctuation of the environment, rendering these individuals highly attuned to emotional and physical feedback. Virgo Moons are invited to soften some of their analysis and practice simply feeling their feelings instead.

MERCURY IN VIRGO: Quick-footed Mercury is the zodiac's butterfly, ruling perception, communication, and how we relate to everyday change. As one of the natural rulers of the sign, Mercury in Virgo delights in sorting and ordering, assimilating information rapidly and deciding what is most vital to the whole. Mercury in Virgos are asked to care delicately for their buzzy nervous systems and to notice when critique has trumped compassion.

VENUS IN VIRGO: Pleasure-petaled Venus rules all kinds of receiving, from money to food to sex. It describes how we take in the world, content to magnetize rather than force our mojo. In Virgo, Venus bows down devotedly to pleasure, eager to bring breakfast in bed to their beloveds. Their growth lies in self-pleasuring, remembering that they have every right to relish the deliciousness of their own lives.

MARS IN VIRGO: Mars is our red-hot muscle and mojo, the source of both our sexuality and success drive. Placed in Virgo, Mars is a carefully oiled ride, checking under the hood and tuning up before hitting the open road. Growth happens when this sign placement remembers that sometimes not everything has to be just right to be unleashed, and that they can step out from beyond the scenes to claim their place among the stars.

JUPITER IN VIRGO: Jupiter is the planet that blows open our windows and doors, beckoning us to expand beyond our constrictive beliefs, and risk connecting to our wild natures. Placed in Virgo, Jupiter is expanding our capacity to contribute in the world, asking us to raise our threshold for devotion and to see both the detailed dirt and the stars above. This sign placement gets lucky when they remember to attend to every last piece of the puzzle, leaving no stone unturned.

SATURN IN VIRGO: Saturn is the planet of limits and laws, a sometimes hard-knocks school that paves the way toward lasting competence. Saturn placed in Virgo asks us to consider our relationship to effort and to check any urges to blindly keep "doing" when we're invited to just "be" instead. A serious sign placement that knows how to get the work done, growth comes from occasionally floating downstream.

URANUS IN VIRGO: This rule-breaker and change-maker is here to shake it up, interrupting our usual societal pro-gramming and urging us to travel beyond the mapped roads. In Virgo, the revolution starts at home, and this placement is encouraged to adopt an innovative approach to caring for themselves and their bodies. Also here to interrupt rote status quo machinery, Uranus in Virgos must commit to finding their own distinctive cause rather than simply toeing the line.

NEPTUNE IN VIRGO: A generational planet that shifts signs every fourteen years, Neptune is the zodiac's dream queen, an escape hatch that takes us into the mystical world and symbolizes where we crave transcendence. Bringing the heaven principle down into the dirt, this sign placement is here to connect us to the magic in every grain of sand. Neptune in Virgo is also encouraged to pay close attention to the direction of their devotion, making sure that where they place their faith and effort is loving them right back.

PLUTO IN VIRGO: The outermost generational "planet," Pluto is ruler of the underworld, a jet-black metal detector of where we must enact karmic change. Pluto in Virgo's intensity is centered on the creative process, amplifying the sign's search for their specialness and expertise. Here to undo some of the expectations about what work looks like, Pluto in Virgos are here to respond to their own rhythms, unleashing the sign's lone wildness by reclaiming places where they've given away their power.

CHIRON IN VIRGO: This touchy-feely planetoid is ready for healing, asking us to develop deep sensitivity and awareness in its sign placement, without having to fix. Placed in the sign of the zodiac's notorious fixer, Chiron in Virgo is cultivating greater allowing in this lifetime, walking alongside their emotions and tempering any harsh urges to "move on" or "get better." Body consciousness is intensified, and healing happens when they explore their own right to humanness, diving into the beautiful mess.

THE NORTH OR SOUTH NODE IN VIRGO: The Nodal axis connects us to past lives and future promises, as we're asked to integrate both our North and South Node signs to come closer to our soul's purpose. With one of the Nodes in Virgo and the other in Pisces, this placement is learning how to balance matter and spirit, blending the urge to merge into the mystically unseen world with the solitary work of incarnating in a body and acknowledging separation.

No planets marked by Virgo? You can still access Virgoan witchery . . .

The House Ruled by Virgo

Check out the pie slices of your chart and look for the Virgo symbol. This is the arena of life in which you're invited to take a Virgoan approach, enacting deeper care, attention, and discernment, and living in alignment with your own code.

The Sign Ruling the Sixth House

The sixth house is naturally ruled by Virgo and awakens the holistic connection between our bodies and our environments. The sign that rules this house in your chart reveals how to approach your daily routine and uncovers where you can apprentice yourself to the process, becoming an experiential learner without having to know it all.

Your Mercury Sign

This cosmic butterfly reveals how we assimilate information, perceive the world, attune our nervous systems to input/output, and relate to everyday change. Look to your Mercury sign to discover how you can more clearly communicate, find your love of learning and field of expertise, and adjust your approach, meeting transitions with more ease.

Your Vesta Sign

This superspecial asteroid is the zodiac's internal, eternal flame keeper. In our charts, Vesta connects us to the territory that is ours and ours alone, showing us how we draw ourselves back to center, apply devotion, and tend our own creative and sensual fires.

Virgo Season

As the sun travels through the entire zodiac, spending about a month in each astrological sign, we all have the opportunity to celebrate and integrate these twelve powerful archetypes. During Virgo season, which signals the final throes of summertime in the Northern Hemisphere, we are starting to harvest the juicy fruits of our labors. It's a time to right our internal rhythms, recommit to our distinctive contribution, and relish all of the untamable tasties we've grown with our own two gorgeous, perfectly imperfect, human hands.

INDEX

ABOUT THE AUTHOR

BESS MATASSA is a New York-based astrologer and tarot reader with an Aries Sun, a fluffy little Leo Moon, and honorary Virgo status due to a planetary pack hanging out in her witchy sixth house. After completing a PhD, she went rogue and started bringing heaven to earth through customized cosmic experiences ranging from birth chart walking tours to zodiac perfume making classes and tarot dance parties. She is the coauthor of *The Numinous Astro Deck* (Sterling, 2019), the author of *Zodiac Signs: Leo* (Sterling, 2020), and has been a cosmic consultant for brands and platforms including *Teen Vogue, PureWow, Apartment Therapy,* and Almay cosmetics. Bess serves up mystical self-inquiry with a side of play, poetry, and pop music, harnessing the language of the cosmos to bring us deeper into the vivid world that surrounds us, and the luscious, lovable selves we already are.

OTHER BOOKS IN THIS SERIES